Harvard
Business
Review

ON

LEADERSHIP AT THE TOP

D0048267

THE HARVARD BUSINESS REVIEW PAPERBACK SERIES

The series is designed to bring today's managers and professionals the fundamental information they need to stay competitive in a fast-moving world. From the preeminent thinkers whose work has defined an entire field to the rising stars who will redefine the way we think about business, here are the leading minds and landmark ideas that have established the *Harvard Business Review* as required reading for ambitious businesspeople in organizations around the globe.

Other books in the series:

Harvard Business Review Interviews with CEOs

Harvard Business Review on Advances in Strategy

Harvard Business Review on Becoming a High Performance Manager

Harvard Business Review on Brand Management

Harvard Business Review on Breakthrough Leadership

Harvard Business Review on Breakthrough Thinking

Harvard Business Review on Building Personal and Organizational Resilience

Harvard Business Review on Business and the Environment

Harvard Business Review on the Business Value of IT

Harvard Business Review on Change

Harvard Business Review on Compensation

Harvard Business Review on Corporate Ethics

Harvard Business Review on Corporate Governance

Harvard Business Review on Corporate Responsibility

Harvard Business Review on Corporate Strategy

Harvard Business Review on Crisis Management

Harvard Business Review on Culture and Change

Harvard Business Review on Customer Relationship Management

Harvard Business Review

ON

LEADERSHIP AT THE TOP

A HARVARD BUSINESS REVIEW PAPERBACK

The *Harvard Business Review* articles in this collection are available as individual reprints. Discounts apply to quantity purchases. For information and ordering, please contact Customer Service, Harvard Business School Publishing, Boston, MA 02163. Telephone: (617) 783-7500 or (800) 988-0886, 8 A.M. to 6 P.M. Eastern Time, Monday through Friday. Fax: (617) 783-7555, 24 hours a day. E-mail: custserv@hbsp.harvard.edu

Library of Congress Cataloging-in-Publication Data
Harvard business review on leadership at the top.
    p.   cm. — (The Harvard business review paperback series) A collection of articles previously published in the Harvard business review. Includes index.
    ISBN 1-59139-275-6 (alk. paper)
    1. Leadership. 2. Chief executive officers. 3. Executives. I. Harvard business review. II. Series.
HD57.7.H3873 2003
658.4'092—dc21   2003008220
                                                                 CIP

The paper used in this publication meets the requirements of the American National Standard for Permanence of Paper for Publications and Documents in Libraries and Archives Z39.48-1992.

Contents

Harvard Business Review

ON

LEADERSHIP AT THE TOP

The Curse of the Superstar CEO

RAKESH KHURANA

Executive Summary

WHEN STRUGGLING COMPANIES look for a new chief executive today, the one quality they prize above all others is charisma. But once they've recruited a larger-than-life leader, they often find that their troubles only get worse. Indeed, as the author's new research painfully reveals, the widespread belief in the powers of charismatic CEOs can be problematic.

Why?

First, Khurana says, there's no conclusive evidence that charismatic leadership affects an organization's performance. And yet—as Kodak's story over the past decade reveals—when a company is faltering, boards feel compelled to oust the incumbent chief executive and bring in a corporate savior.

Second, the insistence on finding a charismatic leader, combined with the undefinable nature of charisma, results in selection processes that are overly conservative and even irrational. Boards end up considering only candidates who have already achieved the rank of CEO or president at a high-performing, high-profile company, even if they are not right for the job.

Third, charismatic leaders deliberately destabilize organizations. This can result in a more vibrant company, as it did at General Electric during Jack Welch's tenure, but it can also leave a troubled legacy for the organization to overcome, as GE, Ford, and Enron have all found.

Faith in a company, a product, or an idea can unleash tremendous innovation and productivity. But the extravagant hopes invested in charismatic CEOs resemble not mature faith but a belief in magic. If we are willing to reconsider our notion of leadership, this age of faith can be followed by an era of faith and reason.

THE SECRET TO BEING A SUCCESSFUL CEO today, it's almost universally assumed, is leadership. Such qualities as strategic thinking, industry knowledge, and political persuasiveness, though desirable, no longer seem essential. Particularly when a company is struggling, directors in the market for a new CEO—as well as the investors, analysts, and business journalists who are watching their every move—will not be satisfied with an executive who is merely talented and experienced. Companies now want leaders.

But what makes a successful leader? When people describe the qualities that enable a CEO to lead, the word they use most often is "charisma." Biographers and journalists have spilled much ink trying to deconstruct the charisma of superstar CEOs such as Lee Iacocca, Jack

Welch, and Steve Jobs. Nevertheless, charisma remains as difficult to define as art or love. Few who advocate it are able to convey what they mean by the term. Fewer still are aware that the concept is borrowed from Christianity. In a passage from the New Testament, the apostle Paul lists the various *charisms,* or gifts of the Holy Spirit, that Christians may possess. According to Paul, those gifted with charisma in this sense include "good leaders." They also include church members with extraordinary endowments, such as the power to speak in tongues or work miracles.

Of course, the meaning of charisma has changed since Saint Paul's time, but there is a lingering sense of admiration—even worship—for the few who are thought to possess uncommon inspirational powers. We now think of charisma as a set of personal qualities that inspire awe and submission in others. Jeffrey Garten, dean of the Yale School of Management, vividly captured the aura of the charismatic leader in his book *The Mind of the CEO.* Describing his first meeting with C. Michael Armstrong, now the CEO of AT&T, Garten effused that Armstrong "radiated the confidence, enthusiasm, and energy of a seasoned politician . . . You had the sense that if you were making a movie and said, 'Get me a CEO,' to the casting director, he'd give you Michael Armstrong."

In researching CEO successions in large U.S. companies over the last half dozen years, I have found that such rapt responses play a surprisingly significant role in determining who is considered qualified to lead America's great corporations. And I have concluded that the widespread quasi-religious belief in the powers of charismatic leaders is problematic for a number of reasons. First, faith exaggerates the impact that CEOs have on companies. Second, the idea that CEOs must have charisma leads companies to overlook many promising candidates and to consider others who are unsuited for the job. Finally, charismatic leaders can destabilize organizations in dangerous ways. Before taking a closer look at each of these dangers, let's untangle the paradox of just how charismatic leadership has come to be the ideal for American business in an era we like to celebrate as being rational and enlightened.

The Pull of Charisma

Charisma wasn't always as important in business as it is today. For the three decades following World War II—in what has been called the era of managerial capitalism—the typical CEO was an "organization man" who worked his way up the ranks and was no better known to the general public than his secretary or his dentist. All that started to change in the 1980s, when a long-standing decline in corporate profits ushered in today's era of investor capitalism. Senior managers—once viewed as enlightened corporate statesmen—began to be portrayed by disgruntled investors as an insulated, self-interested elite, ill prepared to face the challenges of global competition and rapid technological change. Investors were suddenly looking for CEOs who could shake things up and put an end to business as usual.

This important change coincided with two other shifts. The first was the emergence of an almost religious conception of business, exemplified by the appearance of words such as "mission," "vision," and "values" in the corporate lexicon. The second shift was the rise of so-called populist capitalism, whereby ordinary Americans made investing the country's most popular participatory sport. To serve the public's growing appetite for business news, the mass media greatly expanded coverage of corporate doings, focusing—as always—on personalities and easily comprehensible narratives.

In this environment, a new breed of corporate leader—today's charismatic CEO—began to appear. Lee Iacocca, who was elected chairman and CEO of Chrysler in 1979, will probably go down in history as the first modern example of a charismatic business leader. Soon after Iacocca's turnaround of Chrysler made him a celebrity and even a national hero, Steve Jobs, the New Age wunderkind of Apple Computer, gave a more contemporary spin to Iacocca's brand of inspirational leadership. Revered for his success in introducing people to the personal computer—which he dubbed the Star Wars–like "force" that could guarantee our "freedom"— Jobs created a corporate culture that has become widespread. In this new organization, employees were supposed to work ceaselessly, uncomplainingly, and even for relatively low pay not just to produce and sell a product but to realize the vision of the messianic leader.

The charismatic leader was supposed to have the power to perform miracles—to bring a dying company back to life, for instance, or to vanquish much larger, more powerful foes.

What made these chief executives different from their predecessors, apart from their celebrity status and exaggerated self-importance? For a start, the charismatic CEO was typically—though not invariably—either an entrepreneurial founder or someone who had been brought into the company from the outside. Far from being a predictable organization man, he was expected to offer a vision of a radically different future and to attract and motivate followers for a journey to the new promised land. In keeping with the religious conception of the CEO's role, the charismatic leader was also supposed to have the "gift of tongues," with which he could inspire employees to work harder and gain the confidence of investors, analysts, and the ever skeptical business press. Finally, in all too many cases, the charismatic leader was supposed to have the power to perform miracles—to bring a dying company back to life, for instance, or to vanquish much larger, more powerful foes.

It can, of course, be quite exhilarating for an organization when such a leader appears. Whatever else they may be, charismatic CEOs are not dull. But as many companies have found, there's a downside to superstar CEOs. Like its close relative, romantic love, charisma can be blinding. And the consequences of that blindness can be severe.

The White Knight Trap

Our fervent and often irrational faith in the power of charismatic leaders seems to be a part of our human nature. The charismatic illusion is fostered by tales of white knights, lone rangers, and other heroic figures who rescue us from danger. Major events are easier to understand when we can attribute them to the actions of prominent individuals rather than having to consider the interplay of social, economic, and other impersonal forces that shape and constrain even the most heroic individual efforts. Sociologists and social psychologists refer to this common tendency to overestimate the impact of individuals as the "fundamental attribution error," and American society, with its mythology of frontier heroes, pioneering inventors, and other "rugged individuals," has always been beleaguered by it.

Consider George Washington, America's first charismatic political leader. He had to suppress a movement to name him king—as if he had won the Revolution single-handedly. More recently, Ronald Reagan has been credited with winning the Cold War, and many people believe that Alan Greenspan controls the U.S. economy. Tracing the performance of vast business organizations to the quality and actions of CEOs is yet another example of the magical thinking evident in the fundamental attribution error.

What makes today's profound faith in the charismatic CEO so troubling is the lack of any conclusive evidence linking leadership to organizational performance. In fact, most academic research that has sought to measure the impact of CEOs confirms Warren Buffett's observation that when you bring good management into a bad business, it's the reputation of the business that stays intact. Studies

While charismatic leaders (whether in religion, politics, or elsewhere) may appear at any time, they most often emerge—or are called into existence— during a crisis.

show that various internal and external constraints inhibit an executive's ability to affect a company's performance. Most estimates, for example, attribute anywhere from 30% to 45% of performance to industry effects and 10% to 20% to year-to-year economic changes. Thus, the best anyone can say about the effect of a CEO on a company's performance is that it depends greatly on circumstances.

The misguided assumption that CEOs are all-powerful is the main reason that the tenure of business leaders has grown ever briefer in recent years. If a CEO is responsible for a company's successes, after all, he must also be responsible for its failures. My research clearly shows that directors automatically blame the incumbent CEO when a company performs poorly. Scapegoating is as old as human nature, of course, but my interviews strongly suggest that when corporate performance falters, directors come under enormous pressure to fire the CEO and hire a savior. This finding is consistent with the larger historical truth that while charismatic leaders (whether in religion, politics, or elsewhere) may appear at any time, they most often emerge—or are called into existence—during a crisis.

For an example of how a struggling company can misdiagnose its problems by attributing them all to the CEO—and then pin its hopes on a charismatic successor—consider the case of Kodak over the last decade. In the early 1990s, Kodak's then CEO, Kay Whitmore, was intensely criticized for failing to improve the company's performance. Institutional investors, such as Robert Monks's Lens Investment Management, blamed Whitmore for the company's decline, and Wall Street analysts and the media jumped on the bandwagon to demand that Kodak's board depose Whitmore. In August 1993, the company's directors delivered the beleaguered CEO's head in a highly publicized firing. Two months later, the board announced the appointment of the first outsider chief executive in Kodak's history, George Fisher, who was then CEO of high-flying Motorola.

Kodak's new CEO was greeted with much fanfare and high hopes. After all, Fisher was widely credited with Motorola's strong performance during his tenure. But how much of Motorola's success can truly be attributed to him? In light of the company's problems today, it is apparent that much of its earlier success was due to telecommunications deregulation: Increased competition in local cellular markets and lower retail prices led to a more rapid adoption of Motorola's phones and related technology. And if Motorola's successes were largely the result of broad trends, so were Kodak's failings. The analysts and investors counting on Fisher failed to recognize that Kodak's fundamental problems—most notably, missing the shift from chemical to digital photography—had little to do with the company's executive leadership. Indeed, in the decade before Fisher was brought in, Kodak had been described as having one of the most effective executive teams in the United States.

Nevertheless, when Fisher was signed on, he was hailed as a savior. On the day his hiring was announced, Kodak's stock rose $4.87, to $63.62. But after several years of acquisitions and divestitures, significant investments in Internet technologies and digital photography, and a wholesale turnover of executives, the Kodak of today looks much like the Kodak of 1994: a business that derives most of its profits from chemical film manufacturing and processing, a horse-and-buggy operation in the world of digital photography.

Meanwhile, the company's stock has declined by two-thirds since Fisher was brought in. According to analysts, the reason for the company's continued decline is that Fisher and his recent successor, Daniel Carp, have bungled their opportunities. Certainly, they have made some mistakes—as all chief executives do. Yet Kodak's CEO, or even the rest of the company's senior management, is not the main problem. For all the excitement and optimism that are generated by superstar CEOs, the truth remains that the factors affecting corporate performance are varied, highly nuanced, almost frighteningly complex, and certainly beyond the power of even the most charismatic leader to influence single-handedly. To pretend otherwise is to grossly oversimplify reality in the hope of finding easy answers.

Look Bold, but Play It Safe

Kodak's story is a familiar one in business today: When performance fails, directors feel compelled to oust the CEO and bring in a corporate savior, even if the company's poor performance cannot be attributed to the incumbent. In their search for a new chief executive, directors brush up against a stubborn paradox. On the one hand, they need (or believe they need) to find a dynamic leader who will shatter precedent and take the company in a daring new direction. On the other hand, given the elusive, ultimately undefinable nature of charisma—not to mention the possibility that they may make an unwise choice—they also feel a powerful urge to play it safe.

I have found that when directors narrow the initial pool of candidates (which already consists principally of top executives they already know), they try to resolve their conflicting requirements by focusing on candidates whom outsiders will consider acceptable. As a result, candidates who make it to the final round generally have already achieved the rank of CEO or president and come from high-performing, high-status companies.

To appreciate the conservative—even irrational— nature of this selection process, consider how the board of tool and hardware manufacturer Stanley Works chose its current CEO, John Trani. When I asked various Stanley directors to explain their reasons for hiring Trani, the factor I heard most often was that he had come from General Electric and had worked for Jack Welch. Several directors discussed GE's track record in developing executives. All of them pointed to other former GE executives who were now leading U.S. companies that had improved their performance. The almost sublime illogic of their arguments is captured perfectly in one director's comment: "I can't think of a company of comparable size that has created more value than GE during Welch's tenure." Not one of the directors made any explicit connection between Trani's experiences at GE and the problems facing Stanley. In their eyes, Trani had been imbued with charisma simply through his association with GE and Welch.

There's an important point here: Charisma is commonly assumed to be inherent, not borrowed from other people or conferred by the social milieu. But the reality is very different. Whether in religious, governmental, or business contexts, charisma is much more a social product than an individual trait. In primitive societies, leaders often wore special clothing, masks, and ornaments that conferred on them a larger-than-life appearance that helped create perceptions of their charisma. In monarchies, kings and queens assume charisma through their family heritage, buttressing it with such potent symbols as palaces, robes, and crowns. Large offices, private planes, expensive suits, and other trappings of corporate power perform the same function for CEOs.

In addition to relying on such external markers, charismatic CEOs acquire their hold over others by meeting certain socially constructed criteria about what constitutes a great leader. One of the most powerful of these constructs is the idea that outsiders are particularly well qualified to lead. One director I interviewed made this point in bluntly stating the rationale for recruiting an outsider CEO: "The person coming from the outside has a clear mandate, particularly if he is coming into a troubled situation. He is not beholden to anyone. There are so many constraints on the internally promoted individual. There is so much baggage. Organizational boxes, the people in the boxes, probably half the businesses that were bought now should be chucked. . . . [As an insider], you are part of the process. . . . You turn to an outsider and then you can watch the blood spray. You don't see many examples of internal candidates getting to the top of the system and then laying waste to the existing culture."

The belief in the superiority of outsiders further constrains corporate boards in hiring CEOs. Consider the search that led to the March 2000 appointment of Jamie Dimon as CEO of Bank One. In 1999, Bank One was stumbling in the wake of its recent acquisition of First Chicago NBD. Many of Bank One's problems stemmed directly from the difficulty of melding the operations and cultures of the two banks. As performance declined, a revolt led by board members from the former First Chicago ended with the firing of John McCoy, Bank One's illustrious CEO. Although the former First Chicago directors favored appointing Verne Istock, who had been CEO of First Chicago, other board members wanted someone with greater presence to impress Wall Street. They wanted a superstar. Not surprisingly, the search focused on external candidates, and on one in particular: former Citigroup president Jamie Dimon.

Dimon was already a legendary figure on Wall Street by virtue of his long association with—and dramatic firing by—Sandy Weill, with whom he had built the Citigroup empire. Having spent virtually his entire career as a deal maker on the investment banking side of financial services, Dimon had all the mental quickness and chutzpah essential to success in that world. But those were not the traits traditionally valued in commercial and retail banking. Indeed, in many ways Dimon was a strange choice for an organization such as Bank One. He didn't have much experience with retail banking or credit card operations, two of Bank One's largest businesses—the latter the source of many of the bank's operational problems. Known for his hot temper, Dimon also seemed ill suited to bridge the differences between Bank One's freewheeling, entrepreneurial culture and the far more traditional banking culture of First Chicago.

Despite Dimon's apparent drawbacks, he dazzled Bank One's directors. Following a two-hour presentation he made to the board's search committee, outside director and committee chair John Hall summarized his colleagues' reaction: "Everyone knew he was brilliant, but the presentation showed just how brilliant he was." Another member of the search committee enthused that Dimon was the kind of leader who "would not waste time getting stability and consensus, but instead would do what it took to make us the number one bank . . . Istock, on the other hand, was more consensus-oriented. He felt that Bank One needed to be stabilized and that its executives needed a rest from the turmoil that had resulted from the merger and McCoy's departure."

Clearly, the committee's standards did not reflect a half-century's worth of wisdom about achieving organizational efficiency through rational management. (By what measure, one is tempted to ask, is seeking stability and consensus a waste of time?) Rather, the values at work here stem from a mistaken belief that complex organizational problems can be solved by a charismatic outsider. In the case of Jamie Dimon, the jury is still out. He may succeed; he may not. But one thing is clear: Bank

One's perceived need to usher in change while playing it safe narrowed its sights in the search for a new CEO. The board in effect cheated shareholders by rushing to choose the usual suspect—the bold outsider—even if it meant ignoring better candidates.

The Destructive Impulse

The cult of the outsider is so strong that even when insiders are appointed to the CEO post, they are often people who have assumed the traits of outsiders. GE's Jack Welch and Ford's Jacques Nasser, for example, were both career employees of their respective companies who became known for their willingness to "lay waste" to parts of their organizations. Enron's Jeff Skilling was another longtime insider who claimed the mantle of a charismatic leader. He succeeded in doing so by advancing his audacious vision of transforming Enron from an owner and operator of natural gas pipelines to an "asset-light" new economy company and by converting people to his cause.

The common thread in the stories of these three CEOs—and in the stories of most charismatic leaders, whether they are insiders or outsiders—is that they deliberately destabilize their organizations. In some cases, as with GE, the destabilization can bring much-needed changes and result in a more vibrant company. In other cases, as with Ford, it can do more harm than good. In still other cases, as with Enron, it can be disastrous. In all instances, however, destabilization carries great dangers.

First, consider the problem of CEO succession. Indeed, one of the biggest challenges facing Welch's heir, Jeffrey Immelt, is avoiding constant comparison with his larger-than-life predecessor, even as he is forced to deal with the disappearance of the "Welch effect," which pushed up the company's stock price during Welch's tenure. Even at GE, which is famous for having a formal internal-succession process (although the new CEO is still, in the end, selected by the outgoing one), passing the torch from one leader to the next is fraught with difficulties. Because no chief executive stays in the post forever, any system of authority based on the power of an individual will ultimately be unstable. Organizations that depend on a succession of charismatic leaders are essentially relying on luck.

Jacques Nasser illustrates another danger of charismatic CEOs. On being appointed CEO of Ford in 1999, Nasser was hailed by *BusinessWeek* as a "restless, Lebanese-born outsider," who "early on showed the impatience with Ford's bureaucratic fiefdoms that still fuels him today." The charismatic leader of Nasser's type stands in opposition to the past and in opposition to tradition. This kind of leader proclaims the company's destiny—usually in the form of a seductive vision—and demands that all roadblocks be removed. Today, in the troubled wake of Nasser's two-and-a-half-year reign, Ford is struggling to return to its roots as a high-quality manufacturer and a good employer. Its organization has been damaged not only by the mishandling of the Ford Explorer–Firestone disaster but also by Nasser's counter-cultural focus on things like a forced-curve performance system for employees.

Lastly, the destructive impact of a charismatic leader can be seen in Jeff Skilling's ill-fated career at Enron. In this case, the demands of the leader induced blind obedience in his followers. As we now know, Skilling's abilities as a new economy strategist were considerably over-rated. What he clearly excelled at, however, was motivating subordinates to take risks, to "think outside the box"—in short, to do whatever pleased him. One former Enron executive has described the upper managerial ranks of the company as a "yes-man culture." CFO Andrew Fastow—the alleged designer of the off-the-books partnerships that proved central to Enron's downfall—was so enamored of Skilling that he reportedly named one of his children after him and hired the architect who designed the CEO's Houston mansion to design his house.

Enron's board of directors also bent to the will of its charismatic leader when it agreed to suspend its code of ethics to allow top executives to participate in the off-balance-sheet partnerships. Yet almost to the bitter end, Skilling wowed investors and analysts at gatherings that one analyst likened to revival meetings. As Skilling's example illustrates, charismatic leaders reject limits to their scope and authority. They rebel against all checks on their power and dismiss the rules and norms that apply to others. As a result, they can exploit the irrational desires of their followers. That's because following a charismatic leader involves more than merely acknowledging his skills—it requires full surrender.

Enron may seem like an extreme example, but the list of organizations badly crippled by charismatic CEOs includes some of the most respected names in American business. Xerox under the leadership of Rick Thoman—a top IBM executive whom the Xerox board hoped had caught some of Lou Gerstner's magic—provides a particularly sad example. Michael Armstrong's performance at the helm of AT&T thus far has not been much more inspiring. Time and again over the past 20 years, corporate boards have seen the superstars they had hoped would be saviors turn into black holes that sucked the energy and purpose out of their organizations.

A New Era?

The decades that saw the rise and apotheosis of the charismatic CEO were not notable for skepticism. In the 1980s, Ronald Reagan convinced Americans that they could have lower taxes, increased government spending, and balanced budgets, thus leading the way to the biggest deficits in the nation's history. In the 1990s, a parade of pundits and gurus told us that the Internet was changing all the rules. Venture capitalists poured billions into wing-and-a-prayer enterprises with no serious plans for making money, while ordinary investors drove the Dow Jones and the Nasdaq to unsustainable heights at the behest of analysts who claimed to see a pot of gold at the end of every rainbow. It was, in many respects, an age of faith—a faith that was also expressed in the extravagant hopes and expectations invested in charismatic CEOs.

Today's extraordinary trust in the power of the charismatic CEO resembles less a mature faith than it does a belief in magic.

FAITH IS AN INVALUABLE, even indispensable gift in human affairs. In the realm of religion, it is said to move mountains—scarcely an exaggeration when we consider its power to make people believe in and work for the triumph of good in a world of guilt and sorrow. In the sphere of business, the faith of entrepreneurs,

leaders, and ordinary employees in a company, a product, or an idea can unleash tremendous amounts of innovation and productivity. Yet today's extraordinary trust
in the power of the charismatic CEO resembles less a
mature faith than it does a belief in magic. If, however,
we are willing to begin rethinking our ideas about leadership, the age of faith can be followed by an era of faith
and reason.

Originally published in September 2002
Reprint R0209D

Holes at the Top:

Why CEO Firings Backfire

MARGARETHE WIERSEMA

Executive Summary

WHEN A COMPANY DOES WELL, its CEO is showered with money and adulation. When it does poorly, the CEO gets the blame—and the boot. For better or worse, investors now view chief executives as the primary determinant of corporate performance. But the reality is that most companies perform no better after they dismiss their CEOs than they did in the years leading up to the dismissals. Worse, the organizational disruption created by a rushed firing can leave a company with deep and lasting scars. Far from being a silver bullet, the replacement of a CEO often amounts to little more than a self-inflicted wound.

The blame for such poor results, the author argues, lies squarely with the boards of directors. Boards often lack the strategic understanding of the business necessary to give due diligence to choosing a replacement

19

CEO. Concern over restoring investor confidence quickly—rather than doing what's right for the company—drives the selection process. And all too often, companies continue to be dogged by the same old problems after the new CEOs come on board.

But a good board can make a CEO replacement pay off if its members first develop a better understanding of the business context, worry less about pleasing the investment community and more about a replacement's strategic fit, and take an active role in overseeing the new CEO and the performance and direction of the company. In the long run, such approaches are likely to foster stability at the helm—making it less likely a company will have to fire its CEO in the first place.

In the spring of 1995, Kmart was struggling. Once the largest U.S. retailer, the company had been steadily losing ground to Wal-Mart and other competitors. After posting record sales and profits in 1992, it had experienced eight consecutive quarters of disappointing earnings, and its stock price had dropped 74%. Reacting to relentless pressure from shareholders, the company's board of directors dismissed the CEO, company veteran Joseph Antonini, and with great fanfare brought in outsider Floyd Hall to replace him. The arrival of Hall, a former executive at Target and Grand Union, cheered Wall Street, and the company's beleaguered stock shot up 8%. But the cheering was to prove short-lived. Kmart's downward slide soon resumed, its stock price began to slip further, and in 2000, Hall was replaced with Charles Conaway, another outsider. Less than two years later, the company filed for bankruptcy.

Kmart is an extreme case, but the situation is not an unusual one. The firing of CEOs when performance nose-dives has become commonplace in U.S. business. And it's not hard to understand why. At a time when companies have come to be judged by the valuation of their stock, investors now view chief executives as the primary deter-minant of corporate performance. When companies do well, their CEOs are showered with money, perks, and adulation. When they do poorly, they're given the blame—and the boot. The roster of recently deposed U.S. CEOs is long and growing, including—in addition to Kmart's Antonini and Hall—such names as Coca-Cola's Douglas Ivester, Ford's Jacques Nasser, and Procter & Gamble's Durk Jager. And the trend is now spreading to Europe as well, with high-profile dismissals at Deutsche Telekom, ABB, Swiss Life, Fiat, Vivendi, and Bertels-mann, among others.

But does firing a CEO pay off, or do most companies end up like Kmart, with little or nothing to show for bringing in a new leader? I've been studying that question over the last few years, and what I've found is not encouraging. Most companies perform no better—in terms of earnings or stock-price performance—after they dismiss their CEOs than they did in the years leading up to the dismissals. Worse, the organizational disruption created by rushed firings—particularly the bypassing of normal succession processes—can leave companies with deep and lasting scars. Far from being a silver bullet, the replacement of a CEO often amounts to little more than a self-inflicted wound.

The blame for the poor results, my research indicates, lies squarely with boards of directors. Boards often lack the strategic understanding of the business neces-sary to give due diligence to the CEO selection process.

Consequently, they rely too heavily on executive search firms, which are even less informed about the business than they are. Concern over restoring investor confidence quickly—rather than doing what's right for the company—drives the selection process. And board members' ignorance about the factors that drive company performance undermines their ability to provide strategic oversight after the CEO is dismissed. While boards have become accustomed to firing CEOs, they have not yet become adept at making the dismissals pay off.

The Numbers

Typically a CEO gets fired not because the board has thoughtfully and deliberately concluded that it's time for a change at the top but because investors, concerned about poor performance, demand a change. Board members, who have little idea how to address the underlying problems that got their company into trouble in the first place, seek to appease investors in the short term by handing them the CEO's head on a platter. But firing a CEO is not just a bad solution to a complex, long-term problem. It is also surprisingly ineffective at generating short-term gains.

In my research, I examined all instances of CEO turnover in the 500 largest public companies in the United States during 1997 and 1998. I divided the 83 successions that took place in those two years into three categories—outright dismissal, early retirement, and routine retirement—based on press coverage of the event. Of the 83 successions, 37% were dismissals, 34% were early retirements, and only 29% were routine retirements, occurring because the CEO had reached the mandatory retirement age. Given that "early retirement" is almost always a euphemism for a forced removal from office, as many as 71% of the departures can be considered involuntary—a striking change from traditional practice. Research from the 1980s indicates that the percentage of CEO departures not accounted for by normal, age-related retirements ranged from 13% to 36%.

In another break from tradition, I found that outsiders were brought in to replace CEOs 36% of the time. That's far higher than the 11% to 15% levels of outsider appointments found in studies of succession from the 1970s and early 1980s. And when it came to replacing dismissed as opposed to retiring CEOs, companies chose outsiders a whopping 61% of the time.

So what was the result of all this turnover? Not much, as it turns out. I analyzed the financial performance of companies that had fired their CEOs in three ways. First, I compared company performance in the two years prior to CEO dismissal with performance two years after. Second, I compared performance with industry averages for the same periods. Finally, I compared the performance of companies that had fired their CEOs with the performance of those whose CEOs had retired. I found that companies with CEO dismissals experienced no significant improvement in their operating earnings or their stock performance. Operating earnings (earnings before interest and taxes) as a percentage of total assets averaged 11.2% before dismissal and 11.8% after dismissal—not a statistically significant difference. Return on assets averaged 2.6% before dismissal and 2.4% after, again not statistically significant. Company performance relative to industry average also failed to improve significantly after bringing in a new CEO. And performance lagged behind that of companies with routine CEO successions. I couldn't find a single measure suggesting that CEO

dismissals have a positive effect on corporate performance. (I should note that both outgoing and incoming
CEOs can manipulate earnings numbers. The incumbent
may cut discretionary expenditures to boost reported
earnings; the new CEO may decrease transition-year
earnings, hoping to boost future earnings. In both cases,
the time frame I used is long enough that those manipu-
lations should be inconsequential.) A summary of the
comparisons appears in the exhibit "How CEO Dismissals Affect Company Performance."

One company from my study, AT&T, is a case in
point. In October 1997, the board dismissed Robert
Allen, a 40-year company veteran, and brought in a celebrated outsider, former Hughes Electronics executive
Michael Armstrong. Analysts' expectations of a
turnaround under the charismatic Armstrong led ini-
tially to a near doubling of the company's stock price,
from $47 to $90. However, Armstrong had inherited a
company that was overly dependent on its core long-distance business and faced significant competitive and
technological threats. The company was under pressure
to generate earnings growth by pursuing alternative
market opportunities to supplant the core business.
Unfavorable market dynamics and the costly aftermath
of Armstrong's strategy resulted in a steep decline in
shareholder wealth. AT&T's share price plummeted,
and earnings per share went from $2.44 in 1997 to $0.89
in 2001.

Doomed to Fail?

The firing of a CEO is a traumatic event in the life of any
company. For it to be successful, the board of directors
has to guide the process with skill and assurance. Unfor-

tunately, that rarely happens. Most boards fail to provide the leadership required—and that, as much as anything else, accounts for the poor results of CEO dismissals. In examining the experiences of the companies in my study, I uncovered four reasons why boards' actions—or inactions—doom most dismissals to failure.

THE DISMISSAL SETS OFF A CRISIS

Attuned to the lack of investor confidence in the company's leadership, many boards take the path of least resistance and dismiss their CEOs. But the pressure doesn't stop there. The investment community wants a replacement CEO who's both promising and reassuring—and they want him fast.

Because board members are reacting to external pressure, they don't take the time to plan next steps before the dismissal occurs. And they find, after the dismissal, that the corporate organization is completely unable to help them identify a successor. Most large companies do have a reasonable executive succession-planning process in place—but it has one fatal flaw. The process is controlled and orchestrated by the incumbent CEO, which means that it's utterly useless

Directors rarely hear about the fierce disagreements over strategic direction that take place among members of the management team.

if that CEO has just been fired. Extraordinary though this might sound, given how often CEOs are dismissed, boards don't take an active role in normal CEO succession planning, and companies don't make backup succession plans that acknowledge the possibility of an abrupt dismissal.

Suddenly, the directors have a big job to do all by themselves—a job that they have neither the time nor the expertise to do well. Board members usually hold demanding positions elsewhere; more than half are CEOs

How CEO Dismissals Affect Company Performance

When performance sags, boards all too often succumb to investor pressure and fire CEOs, looking for quick gains in earnings or stock-price returns. But as these charts show, company performance following these high-profile dismissals is almost always disappointing.

Company Performance Before and After CEO Firing

Investors today view chief executives as the primary determinant of company performance, yet most companies perform no better after they fire their CEOs than they did in the years leading up to the dismissals.

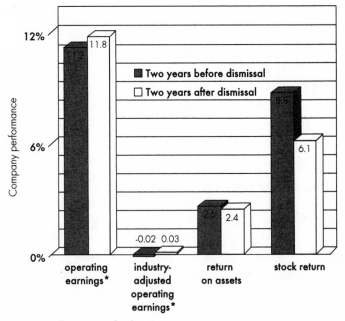

* as a percent of total assets

Company Performance After CEO Firing Versus Routine Succession

Companies that fire their CEOs not only fail to boost their earnings, they also do worse than companies that replace their CEOs in a routine succession process.

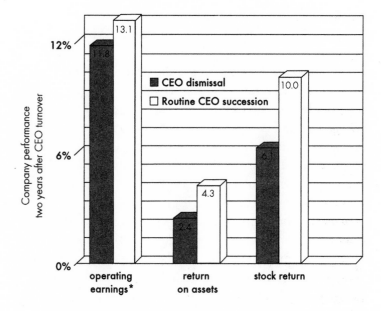

themselves. Nobody's able to make the search process into a full-time effort. The board, knowing that the investment community lacks patience, feels pressure to choose a replacement within three or four months. Typically, they turn the job over to an executive search firm. That would be a reasonable thing to do if the board were prepared to advise recruiters about the unique circumstances in which the company finds itself. Unfortunately, very few board members are able to give recruiters that

kind of advice—which is the second reason most CEO
firings and replacements are doomed to fail.

THE BOARD ISN'T EQUIPPED TO COPE
WITH THE CRISIS

The sad fact is that few board members fully understand
the businesses they supposedly oversee. In good times,
they attend quarterly meetings, absorb the reports that
the CEO prepares, give their approval to strategic initiatives, and leave. The CEO screens all the information
they receive and controls the meeting agenda, which
means that board members are unaware of many of the
complex challenges the company faces and lack sufficient information to actively question the firm's direction or performance. Many critical decisions are never
aired before the board. Directors rarely hear about the
fierce disagreements over strategic direction that take
place among members of the management team, for
example; they hear only what the CEO wants them to
hear after the disagreements have been resolved.

Because board members don't have a detailed understanding of the fundamental problems underlying the
company's competitive deterioration, they can give a
search firm only vague advice about what's needed in
a new CEO. Essentially, they throw the job over the
wall and wait to find out who's available and interested.
The search firm, lacking direction in identifying the
attributes an executive must have to turn the company
around, brings in candidates who have been successful in
the past but may have no particular knowledge of the
company's industry or competitive situation. The board
members don't see any problems with the candidates
because they don't have any particular attributes in

mind themselves. Indeed, at this stage they're not even thinking very clearly about what the company needs— and that's the third problem.

INVESTORS' CONCERNS DRIVE CEO SELECTION

Boards typically pay more attention to pleasing the investment community than they do to fixing the company during the CEO selection process. Analysts' stock valuations are driven in part by their confidence in the CEO. It's natural for board members to want to restore confidence—and stock prices—by appointing a CEO who will appeal to investors.

The desire to please (or appease) the investment community leads board members to choose a candidate who promises a quick fix, usually an outsider they hope will magically turn the company around. They barely consider internal candidates, partly because the investment community likes it that way, partly because any insider is, in a sense, guilty by association. The investment community welcomes the outsider, who supposedly represents a break with the past, by temporarily pushing up the company's stock price. The recent appointment of outsider Richard Notebaert as CEO of Qwest, for example, resulted in a 20% increase in the value of the stock in one day.

But external candidates are often less likely than insiders to understand the company's problems. Consider the case of George Fisher, who became CEO of Kodak in 1993 after Kay Whitmore was dismissed because of financial concerns. Fisher, the former Motorola chairman, adopted a growth strategy and invested heavily in new technology markets—mainly digital photography—while divesting noncore assets. Investors, assuming that Fisher's strategy would pay off, pushed up the stock price and P/E ratio. The company's actual operating earnings improved only slightly, however. Meanwhile, in its core film business—which still represented 80% of sales—Kodak was the high-cost producer despite considerable scale advantages. Fisher stayed focused on his strategy of growth through technology and put almost no pressure on manufacturing plants to improve efficiency. Fuji, Kodak's main competitor in this market, successfully launched an aggressive, price-based attack. The profitability of the core film business was seriously eroded—and Fisher's strategy of expanding the technological base never did result in the contribution to sales and earnings that he'd hoped for. Fisher's experience in the growth-oriented, technology-driven world of cell phones, pagers, and semiconductors made him ill-suited to the mature and increasingly cost-pressured business of photographic film.

BOARDS FAIL TO UNDERSTAND WHICH ISSUES DRIVE PERFORMANCE

Poorly performing companies don't get that way because of any single decision or for that matter any single leader. Patterns of historical decisions, strategic neglect, and misallocation of resources all contribute to the deterioration in performance; some contributing factors may even lie outside the company's control. Board members rarely have a deep understanding of those patterns and forces, which means that they can't provide sufficient oversight going forward or effectively evaluate the performance of the replacement CEO.

Toys R Us exemplifies the difficulty of turning around a deteriorating competitive position without first analyzing the underlying causes. When Robert Nakasone was thrust into the CEO role in 1998, replacing incumbent Michael Goldstein, he took over a company facing several major threats to its profitability and viability. The market it had once monopolized was under direct attack by the discount retailers. In the 1990s, Wal-Mart, which had historically avoided the low-margin toy business, started to aggressively promote the most popular toys as loss leaders to build traffic. Not only that, technology had transformed the nature of toys and entertainment for the older-child market. Computers and electronic games had become toy substitutes, markets in which Toys R Us did not compete. As a result, the company's core toy business was shrinking and becoming ever less lucrative: Market share declined from 25.4% in 1990 to 16.8% in 1998.

Nakasone was under considerable pressure from the board to show that the company was on the right track. As CEO, he undertook significant cost reductions by closing underperforming stores, slashing inventories, and cutting the workforce to improve earnings. His operational improvements, however, did not solve the company's fundamental problems: new competitors in the toy business and technological substitution of toys. Unable to stem further declines in the company's competitive position and faced with a 45% stock price decline during his 18-month tenure, Nakasone, too, was forced out. Because the board was blind to the real challenges facing Toys R Us, it was unable to provide the strategic direction necessary to reap any benefits from new leadership.

A Blueprint for Success

Although many companies fail when it comes to replacing a CEO, not all do. Boards that manage the task effectively tend to have three things in common: They understand that selecting a CEO is a major responsibility, one that's theirs alone; they help the CEO set realistic performance expectations; and they develop a deep understanding of the company's strategic position.

TAKE THE RESPONSIBILITY SERIOUSLY

During the succession process, the board should let strategic needs dictate selection criteria for the new CEO. That's not always easy to do; board members have a tendency to become starstruck. This happens partly because they're trying to please the investment community, but it also happens because they, like investors, imagine that an outsider's charisma or past experience will trump his lack of knowledge about the company or the industry. To circumvent this problem, smart boards first identify the market, competitive, and technological factors that influence the company's performance. If members keep these factors in mind, they'll be better able to identify the skills and experiences that the new CEO will need.

Home Depot's recent CEO replacement process provides a good example of how this should be done. Ken Langone, the board's lead director, was acutely aware that the market and business had evolved in important ways. After two decades of spectacular growth, the company had reached a plateau. Big-box home improvement stores were beginning to look like any other mature business; slower growth and inroads by competitors had started to erode profit margins. Langone and other directors recognized that the founders had outgrown the business and that the company needed a new leader with experience improving efficiency and service. With this in mind, Langone suggested a candidate he knew from his service on GE's board. Bob Nardelli, the former CEO of GE Power Systems, was a talented executive with exactly the kind of experience Home Depot needed. Cofounders and directors Bernie Marcus and Arthur Blank quickly realized the match between Nardelli's credentials and the strategic challenges the company faced. Nardelli proved to be the right choice. Despite flat sales and a declining stock price due to the general economic slowdown, the company is beginning once again to deliver on earnings by taking cost out of the business. Had Langone and the other directors failed to identify the specific attributes required of the new CEO, they likely would never have considered Nardelli—who had virtually no retail experience—for the job.

Even when companies use search firms to find candidates, board members still must first identify the company's competitive challenges and industry context, as well as the skills a replacement CEO will need. Doing so will allow them to guide (rather than be guided by) the recruiters. And it will ensure that recruiters look for a specific set of skills and experiences, rather than simply run through their Rolodexes of available executives.

SET REALISTIC PERFORMANCE EXPECTATIONS

During the economic expansion of the 1980s and 1990s, the investment community came to expect constant improvement in earnings, and most executives and

boards were willing to prop up their stock prices by setting targets that pleased Wall Street. Though it's now
clear that this practice has created serious problems for
corporate America, the pressure from investors lingers.
New CEOs are often tempted to continue playing this
earnings game by promising unrealistic turnaround
numbers, but that's precisely the wrong thing to do.
Instead, the CEO needs to restart the clock by deflating
unrealistic expectations, and the board needs to support
that shift.

James Kilts was quick to reset expectations when he
was appointed CEO at Gillette in January 2001. In his
first meeting with analysts in June of that year, Kilts lam-
basted the unrealistic earnings forecasts set by Michael
Hawley, his predecessor. Hawley had done everything
possible to return Gillette to the 15% to 20% earnings
growth it delivered during the 1990s. "Everything possible" included shortsighted practices such as channel
stuffing—that is, shipping inventory ahead of consump-
tion to meet overblown sales and earnings goals. Despite
these practices (or perhaps because of them), the company was unable to deliver on the numbers, and the
investment community lost confidence in Hawley.

Kilts believed that Gillette's managers were making
decisions based on those looming earnings forecast,
rather than on long-term strategic thinking. So, with the
support of the board, he refused to provide the investment community with any financial targets at all, except
for that of long-term sales growth of 3% to 5%. He told
analysts that he and the board had decided not to give
them guidance going forward. His refusal to play the
game left the investment community perplexed; three
analysts downgraded the stock, and only five out of 17
rated it a buy. Kilts stuck to his guns and focused his

attention on the problems that had led to the earnings
shortfalls. Analysts eventually noted that Gillette's product lines were rebuilding market share, and their confidence in the company's performance began to be
restored. Recent earnings reports show that Gillette's
strategy is beginning to pay off, and the stock has
rebounded from its low.

The point isn't to starve the investment community of
information—far from it. Though the wise board and
CEO will back away from forecasts they can't meet,
they'll also work extremely hard at communicating how
they plan to address underlying competitive problems.
After Jacques Nasser was dismissed from Ford, for example, William C. Ford, Jr., sent strong signals to investors.
With advice and support from the board, he removed the
executives perceived as responsible for Ford's problems.
He also attempted to restore confidence in the company's
finances by appointing for-
mer Wells Fargo Bank chairman and CEO Carl Reichardt
as vice chairman, with the
specific responsibility of
overseeing Ford Financial. Then he announced a sweeping restructuring that trimmed production, rationalized
car lines, reduced purchasing costs, and cut the labor
force. These actions communicated the direction he and
the board envisioned for the company more than any set
of forecasted numbers could have done.

*Once board members
appoint a new CEO,
their job is far from over;
they must be more
vigilant than ever.*

PROVIDE MORE STRATEGIC OVERSIGHT

And finally, good boards develop a deep understanding
of the business and apply that understanding through

active oversight of strategic performance. Once board members have appointed a new CEO, their job is far from over. They must resist the temptation to leave well enough alone for a while and remember that, since most replacement CEOs perform no better than their predecessors, they must be more vigilant than ever.

It's essential that boards provide strong strategic oversight following a dismissal because turnarounds aren't easy. They take subtlety, sophistication, and staying power. Consider General Motors. For nearly a decade under the leadership of Roger Smith, GM put profits ahead of sales—and watched its U.S. market share decline from 45% in 1980 to 36% in 1990. Eventually, the decline in market share eroded financial performance, and, despite the appointment of a new CEO, Robert Stempel, GM suffered losses in 1990 and 1991. The problems clearly went far beyond top leadership. GM offered too broad a range of product lines; the lines didn't share platforms or components; too many components were manufactured internally at higher costs; and the supply chain wasn't managed aggressively. Perhaps most important, central-office bureaucracy consistently stifled GM's ability to become a more innovative and efficient organization.

Following the back-to-back losses, Stempel, too, was dismissed, and the company finally got serious about turning itself around. The board appointed John F. Smith, Jr., who ultimately engineered GM's comeback. The board had to learn to be patient; the problems that had developed over a decade could not be solved particularly overnight. Performance didn't improve much while Smith, with close oversight from the board, directed the much-needed overhaul: aggressively reducing costs through car platform rationalization, manufacturing consolidation, and outsourcing; spinning off the electrical components group, Delphi Automotive; selling aerospace business GM Hughes to Raytheon; and fundamentally restructuring the way the company conducted its business. Ultimately, GM improved its domestic and international operations and was rewarded with an increase in market share and a rebound in stock price. But that turnaround took almost a decade to accomplish—and it likely would never have happened at all if the board hadn't developed a sophisticated understanding of the complex, interconnected problems GM faced.

To ensure that they are providing proper oversight, board members should request from the CEO a strategic plan that identifies the options to consider, a timetable for a turnaround, most likely outcomes, and measures for evaluating whether the company is on track. Board members should closely question the assumptions underlying the strategic plan and how the proposed strategy alters the firm's risk factors and shapes its future direction. They should be willing to act if the new CEO does not improve the company's position in the marketplace. Despite the understandable desire to give the new CEO an extended honeymoon, members won't have fulfilled their primary fiduciary duty unless they formalize the responsibility to oversee strategy.

Target's board has figured out a way to fulfill its oversight function responsibly and constructively. The board formally reviews the CEO, and his or her progress on the strategic plan, every year. The chairman of the board encourages directors to make detailed inquiries, particularly when the company does not appear to be on track. The process is rigorous, but it's also very open; both the board and the executive team benefit from reviewing strategic assumptions together and debating strategic moves before they occur. The board's active oversight means that members are fulfilling their legal responsibility to the shareholders—and it also means they're giving the CEO far more feedback than most CEOs get. In the long run, this type of process is likely to foster stability at the helm since it encourages debate and questioning before a crisis emerges. The stronger the board, in other words, the less likely it is a company will have to fire its CEO in the first place.

THE BOARD AND THE CEO share responsibility for corporate performance, so it stands to reason that when a CEO fails, the board has failed as well. A good board will shoulder its share of the responsibility and commit to more diligent oversight in the future. Practically speaking, that means developing a better understanding of the business context; worrying less about pleasing the investment community and more about strategic fit when choosing a replacement; insisting on richer, fuller briefings from the new top-management team; and taking an active role in overseeing the CEO and the strategic performance of the company.

Originally published in December 2002
Reprint R0212E

A Letter to the Chief Executive

JOSEPH FULLER

Executive Summary

BEYOND THE RECENT ACCOUNTING scandals, something is wrong with the way most companies are managed today. That's the message of this fictional letter from
a board member to a CEO, written by Joseph Fuller, CEO
of strategy consulting firm the Monitor Group.

The letter highlights the challenges and complexities
of running a business in today's uncertain environment.
And while it avoids the facile bashing of U.S. executives
so common these days, the missive nonetheless casts a
harsh light on the flaws that have recently been exposed
in the American management model.

The letter addresses a single CEO and company, yet
it is intended to speak to executives and boards every-
where:

It wasn't the recession that caused us to make three
acquisitions in two years at very, very high prices; the

need to fuel [unreasonable] growth did. Nor was it the recession that caused us to expand our capacity in anticipation of gaining market share; rather, it was our own overly optimistic sales forecasts that led us to that decision. Where did those forecasts originate? From line managers trying to fulfill profit goals that we created after meeting with the analysts.

"The root cause of many of the problems that became apparent in the last 24 months lies not with the economy, not with September 11, and not with the dot-com bubble. Rather, it lies with that willingness to be led by outside forces—indeed, our own lack of conviction about setting a course."

Restoring sound, strategic decision making—thinking that looks beyond tomorrow's analyst reports—will go a long way toward keeping those outside forces at bay, according to Fuller.

Editors' Note: *This fictional letter from a board member to a CEO highlights the challenges and complexities of running a business in today's uncertain environment. While avoiding the facile bashing of U.S. executives so common these days, it nonetheless casts a hard light on the flaws that have recently been exposed in the American management model. We hope that you find it an illuminating, and bracing, read.*

Dear CEO,

I'VE BEEN REFLECTING ON the recent board meeting. We were all encouraged by the third-quarter revenue numbers and the improving forecast for the year. The stabilization of our gross margin, despite the price cuts, speaks well of your latest cost reduction initiatives. On the whole, I think we can safely assume we've weathered the current storm. However, while we can all be grateful for the recent signs of an upturn in our performance, I suspect the next year or two will hold many challenges.

Indeed, the stabilization of our situation offers only a brief reprieve, if any at all. Like many companies these days, we have a workforce that remains fragile after surviving rounds of layoffs. We operate in an industry that still has decidedly too much capacity. And we are embroiled in a market share battle that shows no signs of abating. I'm not sure if anyone really knows which of our competitors started the price war—for all I know, we did—but we've only just begun to see the effects on margins and market share. Furthermore, some of our competitors' recent earnings restatements and their use of "creative" accounting will surely bring more scrutiny to our company in the months ahead. In short, you'll have your hands full indefinitely.

That is precisely why I'm writing to share some thoughts on a less obvious, but nonetheless critical, issue: your role as the leader of the company during this time of uncertainty. I know I risk sounding like every pundit in America when I raise these issues, but I want to talk to you openly about your role and responsibilities in the future. I think my long service on the board and those years we spent working together on the industry council have earned me that right. Or perhaps, merely your indulgence.

I will spare you a sermon on the need for integrity in our financial reporting. I must admit, however, that even by the jaded standards of someone who has served as a director of public companies for more than 15 years, I'm shocked by what we've witnessed in the last several years. As the chair of the Audit Committee, I remain satisfied both with the accuracy of our financial reporting and the performance of our auditors. Similarly, I'm not concerned about the level of your compensation or dealing in our stock. Nonetheless, we must guard against even the appearance of rapaciousness or self-dealing, lest we invite intense scrutiny from the business press, the union, and institutional investors.

This risk is just one way in which the current circumstances have thrust you into a position where your actions will have a disproportionate impact on the company's prospects. As the famous World War II admiral Bull Halsey once said, "There are no great men, only great challenges that ordinary men are forced by circumstances to meet." I think the next couple of years will offer those "great challenges" and will require all your skill to meet them. Another observation: Whether you like it or not, your career is apt to be judged by your performance over that period.

As you know, I've watched this industry closely for many years—seven of them as a CEO myself—and this isn't the first downturn I've seen. As I've thought about it, though, I've come to reject most of the analogies between this and previous recessions as flawed. In my view, the most important feature of this recession is what happened in the years preceding it. It was during that time that we fell victim both to our hubris and to the pressures to perform up to Wall Street's expectations instead of our own.

In retrospect, it is now clear that because of our desire to "meet or beat the street," we made a number of strategic choices and instigated a series of changes to the underlying management system that caused us to fall harder and faster than necessary. For example, you and the CFO consistently told the market that we could grow profits at a 15% compound annual rate, even though our core businesses were struggling to hit 4% top-line growth and we were close to exhausting our supply of sensible cost reduction options. Sure, the consultants told us it was possible. And yes, the rest of the board and I got caught up in the rhetoric and went along. But look where that left us when the downturn hit.

After all, it wasn't the recession that caused us to make three acquisitions in two years at very, very high prices (ah, the benefit of hindsight!); the need to fuel that growth did. Nor was it the recession that caused us to expand our capacity in anticipation of gaining market share; rather, it was our own overly optimistic sales forecasts that led us to that decision. Where did those forecasts originate? From line managers trying to fulfill profit goals that we created after meeting with the analysts. Because we bought into the analysts' logic instead of asserting our own, we ended up with unrealistic goals and similarly unrealistic plans to meet them.

We didn't just add marginal plant and equipment, but marginal people as well, right across the workforce. The tight labor market scared us and we overreacted. We had the hiring spigot turned on all the way almost until the day we pulled the plug. No wonder the Internet chat rooms are full of angry comments. We changed the story we were telling employees practically in midsentence. It wasn't the tight labor market, though, that caused us to increase executive compensation and, especially, to award options to everyone at the vice-president level and above. The Compensation Committee did that with the input and encouragement of management. (Again, as a former member of that committee, I have to shoulder some of the blame here.) The liberal granting of options helped create a generation of executives who now think they're entitled to become millionaires.

I'm not saying these decisions and others were necessarily all that wrongheaded at the time. As I reflect on it, however, one thing does stand out. I think we were guilty of focusing more on what others expected of us than on what we knew was the real potential of the company and the real opportunities in our industry. In the last few years, we've defined our strategy more and more in terms of outcomes—How do we grow revenue at this rate, or EPS at that rate?—and less and less around the substantive decisions that actually drive those outcomes—How do we gain leadership in this market, or should we invest in that technology? Driven by the need to meet stretch financial goals, we've invested in plants making products that are only marginally profitable. We've ventured into new markets without asking whether we'll be able to wrest share from rivals who intend to defend their turf as fiercely as we defend ours. In short, we took new initiatives simply because they gave us some hope of making our numbers, not because we were confident that the business logic was sound.

Despite what the headlines say, I think the root cause of many of the problems that became apparent in the last 24 months lies not with the economy, not with September 11, and not with the dot-com bubble. Rather, it lies with that willingness to be led by outside forces— indeed, our own lack of conviction about setting a course. Now that things are settling down a bit, I think you need to take a deep breath and think about how to use this *annus horribilis* as an opportunity to break some bad habits. Specifically, I think you should use it to alter the fundamental nature of the conversations you've been having with some of your key constituencies: Wall Street, the board, the senior executive team, and the rank-and-file workforce. Since last year's performance eliminated any chance of fulfilling the expectations we helped create in each of these constituencies, let's reboot and set expectations that are based on reality.

L ET'S START WITH WALL STREET. During my 15 years on your board, I've watched as the agenda of the board meetings has become more and more focused on the analysts, their expectations, whether we'll meet them, et cetera, et cetera. Until recently, we talked about how to manage these expectations. Even though the SEC has put the kibosh on all the private, in-depth briefings and whispered conversations with analysts, we're still spending too much time figuring out whether and where we'll fall in their expected range. In my view, that's putting the cart before the horse. Too often, last year's "strategic initiatives" have been scrapped in the interest of this quarter's earnings. Investments and acquisitions we had celebrated as major growth vehicles have been pared back, sold, or written off—in response to skepticism from analysts or the rating agencies as much as out of managerial conviction.

What bothers me is that we seem to have lost control of the situation. We spend more time talking about what the analysts think we should earn than we do discussing what the company is capable of earning.

What bothers me is that we seem to have lost control of the situation. We spend more time talking about what the analysts think we should earn than we do discussing what the company is capable of earning. I realize that we have a credenza full of bankers' reports telling us that "high performance" companies grow their earnings at 15% annually. I just haven't seen the corresponding study showing how you do that in a market that is growing in the single digits, with a company that has gone through multiple waves of cost reduction and asset rationalization.

Once upon a time, analysts studied companies in order to understand their potential, describe the case for investing to their clients, and make recommendations. Many of them developed a deep understanding of how particular companies had positioned themselves, how the fundamental economics of an industry worked, and what company-specific risks various players faced. Admittedly, the world and our business have gotten more complicated during my tenure on the board, but it seems to me that many of our current analysts don't have that type of understanding. When news is grim, they always seem shocked, scurrying to rewrite their estimates and relegating companies that surprise them to the "penalty box."

I'm not advocating that we simply do a better job of "investor relations" —at least as the term has been defined in recent years. I'm talking about basing our discussions with analysts on the fundamentals of our business.

Well, our company is in the penalty box now. But it was inevitable, if not this year, then soon. The earnings tightrope was too long and the market winds too high for us to meet their expectations. So let's not fight it. Let's exploit it. I think we should move away from managing the market's expectations and invest more time in building the analysts' understanding of the company and its fundamental economics. That means being much clearer about our strategy, what risks it entails, and what the analysts need to believe about us and our markets to think we're a good investment.

Now let *me* be clear: I'm not advocating that we simply do a better job of "investor relations"—at least as the term has been defined in recent years. I'm talking about basing our discussions with analysts on the fundamentals of our business. At present, we spend most of our time with them trying to predict our quarterly earnings down to the very last penny. Last year, we forecast annual earnings within a range of 20 cents per share. Given the previous year's earnings of $2.25 per share, we were offering a number with roughly a 10% margin of error. How can we make such a forecast when we compete in a global business that has not only normal systemic risks but also competitive, product-liability, and exchange-rate risks, among others?

Instead of engaging in this virtually meaningless exercise, let's give the analysts a better understanding of the progress—or lack thereof—we're making on key strategic initiatives and then link that progress to future financial results. We currently do the opposite, obfuscating what's going on in the business to leave ourselves future flexibility. But if growth in a new product or gaining access to new channels is key to our success, then we need to be more forthcoming about how we're doing. It's not as if the analysts won't find out eventually. And I'm sure we can provide this information with enough discretion to avoid publishing anything a determined competitor couldn't find out independently.

By being more forthcoming, we can get analysts to focus on what we're actually managing—the business— and less on what we can't manage nearly as precisely—

the quarter-to-quarter financial results. It will also relieve them of the burden of surmising the cause-and-effect relationship between our strategy and our financial results—and us of the burden of speaking to them obliquely. If nothing else, the analysts ought to be grateful, given the cloud that hangs over audited financial statements. If we get out in front on this, I think we have a real chance to differentiate ourselves from our competitors.

I THINK YOU'LL FIND an approach that features visible, accurate, and reliable information about corporate performance much more to the liking of the board, too. I've complained to you before that the senior executives seem to treat our strategy reviews with them like a dinner at the in-laws. They're on their best behavior, say as little as possible that might be remotely controversial, and define victory as a clean getaway. I don't think the more experienced directors like the degree to which we have been shut out of substantive discussions. We all know that you're cautious about inviting too much back-and-forth. Indeed, all of us directors run or have run our own outfits and know that too many cooks spoil the soup. But you don't have to substitute pablum for soup. If you adopt the type of discipline I'm suggesting you adopt in your discussions with the Street, you will greatly elevate the quality of the discussions we have in the boardroom. You'll also have a board that adds more value and is more committed to your program.

I should add that, at some point, it doesn't matter what I prefer or what you think about the substance of board meetings. Enron and WorldCom changed everything. I don't know of a single director of a publicly traded company that hasn't reviewed his D&O insurance policies in recent months. No one in his right mind is going to put his reputation at risk by not knowing what is really going on in companies whose shareholders he represents. Just as shareholders should insist on a far clearer line of sight between financial projections and management actions, boards will insist on understanding the links between management decisions and business risk. Your board will certainly be one of them.

Let me turn to the senior executive team. I've been concerned about where these managers have been focusing their attention in recent years. During last spring's off-site, I chatted with many of them. They are bright and motivated, no doubt. However, in my conversations with them, each seemed unduly concerned about this year's budget, making the quarter, and the market's reaction to our recent "negative" earnings guidance.

Now, maybe that's what they thought I wanted to hear. And certainly, when I was in their shoes, I also was cautious about what I brought up with an outside director. But I think it's indicative of a more fundamental, and potentially insidious, problem. If we look at how these folks get paid, it should come as no surprise that they focus on the share price. In recent years, several things have happened. The tolerance for short-term performance problems has become

Through our use of options we've infected top managers with the same type of short-term thinking that was the punch line of every joke about American management 15 years ago.

almost nonexistent. And as an executive team and a board, we have consistently signaled to top managers that they had better make the numbers, or else. Why?

Because we feel we have to make the earnings estimates, or else. And, by loading executives up with options, we guaranteed that they would focus on share-price performance as well.

Certainly, the Compensation Committee eagerly embraced this program as a vehicle for ensuring that executives focus on shareholder value. But I wonder now whether we actually accomplished that purpose. Should these people really be checking the hourly movement of the stock price at the expense of worrying about product marketing, the workforce, and asset utilization? Someday, once they have proven themselves at the business-unit and group-VP levels, they will find it important to monitor the health of the overall corporation, as reflected in the fluctuations in its stock price. For the moment, though, they should focus on those things they control directly.

Furthermore, it would seem to me that through our use of options we've infected top managers with the same type of short-term thinking that was the punch line of every joke about American management 15 years ago, when American executives were criticized for managing by the numbers and lacking any real sense of their business or industry. More importantly, I wonder if we've skewed their expectations. I realize that during the height of the dot-com bubble, everybody and his uncle believed their destiny was to get rich, young. We certainly accelerated the pace of salary and bonus increases to keep the best of our executives, when we feared they would head off to some new-economy start-up. Obviously, that fear has passed. Still, the aftereffects linger.

Don't get me wrong: As you know, I have argued in board meetings that there is a market for executives, and we have to meet that market to keep our top talent. You will credit me, I think, with being an unstinting ally in helping to maintain our position in the top quartile of executive compensation in our industry. While I think that is important, I don't think we should fall into a mindless, keeping-up-with-the-Joneses mentality. Every year, our compensation consultants tell us that the mean has shifted upward; every year, we meet the new standard. And, in recent years, that has meant not only increasing the number of options and broadening the group of recipients but also repricing them when our stock price fell. All of that added up to a huge shift in the expected value of our managers' compensation from salary and bonus to options. But after the battering our stock took during the tumultuous weeks the market experienced in the summer, we've shifted them on to thin ice. At this point, I don't think it's an overexaggeration to say that the fundamental, underlying logic of our executive compensation program is in tatters.

I think we need to revisit the logic of compensation for executives. We have to refocus them on their specific responsibilities by linking their individual rewards more materially to their performance in advancing our strategy. I'm not suggesting that we abandon shareholder value creation as our overarching metric. But I do think we should start deconstructing that metric into component parts that are related to our strategy and reward executives on that basis. Let's embed in the compensation system the same logic we'd like the market to adopt.

Our employees want the company to succeed and, on the whole, are willing to put up with a lot to ensure that outcome. But they have to be given some reason to make that sacrifice.

FINALLY, I BELIEVE WE ARE fooling ourselves if we
think that the issues I have outlined above are lost on the
nonexecutive workforce. Just what have they seen from
us in the last five to ten years? First, they have witnessed
a massive increase in both the reported value of executive pay packages and the amount of press coverage
those packages receive. More importantly, they have
seen a fundamental change in the way we approach the
business. Simply put, they believe we lack commitment
to it—and to them. Many would call us not only selfish
but spineless. New product programs come and go, not
on their merits, but on our ability to fund them year to
year based on earnings requirements. Functions ranging
from IT to internal audit are outsourced, their employees
unceremoniously seconded to new employers like so
many indentured servants. Procurement "rationalization" results in the termination of longtime suppliers.
Overhead cost reduction campaigns, "delayering," and
early retirement incentive packages are followed by a
massive ramp-up in hiring—and then equally precipi-
tous layoffs.

What message do these moves send to our employees? Basically, we're saying: "When the chips are down,
don't count on us." And that's a message that's not only
heartless but dangerous. I believe our employees want
the company to succeed and, on the whole, are willing to
put up with a lot to ensure that outcome. But they have
to be given some reason to make that sacrifice. We no
longer denominate success in building great products or
providing a great place to work, but in cents per share.
Frankly, that is not enough.

Implicit in what I've been saying is the need for you to
rethink how you exercise leadership in this company.
Leading in a time of uncertainty is a fundamentally dif-

ferent task from leading in a time of unquestioned irrational exuberance. If we think about those leaders whose greatness evinces itself in times of trouble, what we remember is their ability to communicate. Their messages always share the same qualities—clarity, consistency, and an underlying moral purpose. Moreover, they demonstrate the integrity of those messages through their actions, setting a course and then staying with it in the face of adversity and opposition. In short, they say what they mean and do what they say.

Their messages may be delivered in the native dialects of their different constituencies; these leaders, after all, know their audiences. But the overarching theme is the same. And it embodies a mission that people can rally around.

Let's face it. You don't motivate people with "Let's knock ourselves out again to make another stretch quarter." As rallying cries go, this isn't exactly, "Once more unto the breach, dear friends!" To inspire people to follow you, to commit themselves to your endeavor, to make needed sacrifices, you have to offer an inspiring mission. It doesn't need to be dramatic, but it does need to be meaningful. I think restoring sound, strategic decision making that looks beyond tomorrow's analyst's report will take us a long way toward a mission of which we can all be proud.

The results will take care of themselves.

Originally published in October 2002
Reprint R0210G

The Very Real Dangers of Executive Coaching

STEVEN BERGLAS

Executive Summary

A PERSONAL COACH TO HELP your most promising executives reach their potential—sounds good, doesn't it? But, according to Steven Berglas, executive coaches can make a bad situation worse. Because of their backgrounds and biases, they ignore psychological problems they don't understand. Companies need to consider psychotherapeutic intervention when the symptoms plaguing an executive are stubborn or severe.

Executives with issues that require more than coaching come in many shapes and sizes. Consider Rob Bernstein, an executive vice president of sales at an automotive parts distributor. According to the CEO, Bernstein had just the right touch with clients but caused personnel problems inside the company. The last straw came when Bernstein publicly humiliated a mail clerk who had interrupted a meeting to ask someone to sign for a package.

At that point, the CEO assigned Tom Davis to coach Bernstein. Davis, a former corporate lawyer, worked with Bernstein for four years. But Davis only exacerbated the problem by teaching Bernstein techniques for "handling" employees—methods that were condescending at best. While Bernstein appeared to be improving, he was in fact getting worse.

Bernstein's real problems went undetected, and when his boss left the company, he was picked as the successor. Soon enough, Bernstein was again in trouble, suspected of embezzlement. This time, the CEO didn't call Davis; instead, he turned to the author, a trained psychotherapist, for help. Berglas soon realized that Bernstein had a serious narcissistic personality disorder and executive coaching could not help him.

As that tale and others in the article teach us, executives to be coached should at the very least first receive a psychological evaluation. And company leaders should beware that executive coaches given free rein can end up wreaking personnel havoc.

OVER THE PAST 15 YEARS, it has become more and more popular to hire coaches for promising executives. Although some of these coaches hail from the world of psychology, a greater share are former athletes, lawyers, business academics, and consultants. No doubt these people help executives improve their performance in many areas. But I want to tell a different story. I believe that in an alarming number of situations, executive coaches who lack rigorous psychological training do more harm than good. By dint of their backgrounds and biases, they downplay or simply ignore deep-seated psychological problems they don't understand. Even more concerning, when an executive's problems stem from undetected or ignored psychological difficulties, coaching can actually make a bad situation worse. In my view, the solution most often lies in addressing unconscious conflict when the symptoms plaguing an executive are stubborn or severe.

Consider Rob Bernstein. (In the interest of confidentiality, I use pseudonyms throughout this article.) He was an executive vice president of sales at an automotive parts distributor. According to the CEO, Bernstein caused trouble inside the company but was worth his weight in gold with clients. The situation reached the breaking point when Bernstein publicly humiliated a mail clerk who had interrupted a meeting to get someone to sign for a parcel. After that incident, the CEO assigned Tom Davis to coach Bernstein. Davis, a dapper onetime corporate lawyer, worked with Bernstein for four years. But instead of exploring Bernstein's mistreatment of the support staff, Davis taught him techniques for "managing the little people"—in the most Machiavellian sense. The problem was that, while the coaching appeared to score some impressive successes, whenever Bernstein overcame one difficulty, he inevitably found another to take its place.

Roughly six months after Bernstein and Davis finished working together, Bernstein's immediate boss left the business, and he was tapped to fill the position. True to his history, Bernstein was soon embroiled in controversy. This time, rather than alienating subordinates, Bernstein was suspected of embezzlement. When confronted, he asked to work with his coach again.

Fortunately for Bernstein, the CEO suspected that something deeper was wrong, and instead of calling Davis, he turned to me for help.

After just a few weeks of working with Bernstein, I realized that he had a serious narcissistic personality disorder. His behavior was symptomatic of a sense of entitlement run amok. It is not at all uncommon to find narcissists at the top of workplace hierarchies; before their character flaws prove to be their undoing, they can be very productive. Narcissists are driven to achieve, yet because they are so grandiose, they often end up negating all the good they accomplish. Not only do narcissists devalue those they feel are beneath them, but such self-involved individuals also readily disregard rules they are contemptuous of.

No amount of executive coaching could have alleviated Bernstein's disorder. Narcissists rarely change their behavior unless they experience extraordinary psychological pain—typically a blow to their self-esteem. The paradox of Bernstein's circumstance was that working with his executive coach had only served to shield him from pain and *enhance* his sense of grandiosity, as reflected in the feeling, "I'm so important that the boss paid for a special coach to help me." Executive coaching further eroded Bernstein's performance, as often occurs when narcissists avoid the truth.

Many executive coaches, especially those who draw their inspiration from sports, sell themselves as purveyors of simple answers and quick results.

My misgivings about executive coaching are not a clarion call for psychotherapy or psychoanalysis. Psychoanalysis, in particular, does not—and never will—suit everybody. Nor is it up to corporate leaders to ensure that all employees deal with their personal demons. My goal, as someone with a doctorate in psychology who also serves as an executive coach, is to heighten awareness of the difference between a "problem executive" who can be trained to function effectively and an "executive with a problem" who can best be helped by psychotherapy.

The issue is threefold. First, many executive coaches, especially those who draw their inspiration from sports, sell themselves as purveyors of simple answers and quick results. Second, even coaches who accept that an executive's problems may require time to address still tend to rely solely on behavioral solutions. Finally, executive coaches unschooled in the dynamics of psychotherapy often exploit the powerful hold they develop over their clients. Sadly, misguided coaching ignores—and even creates—deep-rooted psychological problems that often only psychotherapy can fix.

The Lure of Easy Answers

The popularity of executive coaching owes much to the modern craze for easy answers. Businesspeople in general—and American ones in particular—constantly look for new ways to change as quickly and painlessly as possible. Self-help manuals abound. Success is defined in 12 simple steps or seven effective habits. In this environment of quick fixes, psychotherapy has become marginalized. And executive coaches have stepped in to fill the gap, offering a kind of instant alternative. As management guru Warren Bennis observes, "A lot of executive coaching is really an acceptable form of psychotherapy. It's still tough to say, 'I'm going to see my therapist.' It's okay to say, 'I'm getting counseling from my coach.'"

To achieve fast results, many popular executive coaches model their interventions after those used by sports coaches, employing techniques that reject out of hand any introspective process that can take time and cause "paralysis by analysis." The idea that an executive coach can help employees improve performance quickly is a great selling point to CEOs, who put the bottom line first. Yet that approach tends to gloss over any unconscious conflict the employee might have. This can have disastrous consequences for the company in the long term and can exacerbate the psychological damage to the person targeted for help.

Consider Jim Mirabella, an executive earmarked for leadership at an electronic games manufacturer. Ever since the CEO had promoted him to head of marketing, Mirabella had become impossible to work with. Colleagues complained that he hoarded information about company strategy, market indicators, sales forecasts, and the like. The theory circulating through the grapevine was that Mirabella's aim was to weaken junior executives' ability to make informed contributions during interdivisional strategic-planning sessions. He was assigned an executive coach.

At first meeting, coach Sean McNulty was impressive. He had a bodybuilder's physique and a model's face. Although he had been cocaptain of the football team at the Big Ten university he had attended, McNulty always knew that he was too small for professional sports and not studious enough for medicine or law. But realizing he had charisma to spare, McNulty decided, while an undergraduate business major minoring in sports psychology, that he would pursue a career in executive coaching. After earning an MBA from a leading university, McNulty soon became known in the local business community as a man who could polish the managerial skills of even the ugliest of ducklings.

McNulty's mandate was to shadow Mirabella 24/7 for as long as needed to ensure that he would grow into his position. From the start of their relationship, McNulty and Mirabella had two private meetings a day during which McNulty analyzed Mirabella's behavior and role-played effective styles for mastering interpersonal situations that Mirabella did not handle well. True to his jock background, McNulty reacted to Mirabella's avowals of ineptitude and anxiety with exhortations. "Quitters never win, and winners never quit" was a favorite comment of his, but at times McNulty would also chide Mirabella for being a "weakling" who needed to "act like a man" to deal with the demands of his preordained role within the company.

By dint of McNulty's force of personality or indefatigability, Mirabella stopped fighting his coach's efforts to toughen him up. To all outward appearances, Mirabella began acting like the assertive executive he wasn't. Once McNulty saw Mirabella's behavior change, he told the CEO that Mirabella was now up to the job. But within a week of ending his meetings with McNulty, Mirabella became severely depressed. At that point, he turned to me for help.

I soon realized that Mirabella wasn't trying to sabotage his colleagues in order to get ahead. In fact, he felt he was moving ahead too fast. Mirabella was convinced that he had only been promoted because, like the company's CEO, he was an Italian-American. Mirabella believed that he hadn't earned his success but had it imposed on him because of the CEO's wish for an appropriate heir to the throne. As a result, Mirabella felt enormously anxious and angry. "Why should I be forced to overachieve just so I can fulfill my boss's dream to keep the company in the hands of Italians?" he demanded.

An even more important component of Mirabella's emotional struggle, though, was his morbid fear of failure. He obsessed that the leadership style he had developed belonged to his coach—not to him—and he dreaded being exposed as a fake.

Had Mirabella's coach been less sports driven—or better versed in interpersonal psychology—he could have anticipated that all the learned bravado in the world could never prepare Mirabella for the role he was assigned to fill. Mirabella needed someone who would listen to his fears and analyze their origins. In the end, Mirabella could function effectively only if his advancement was predicated on his own desires and leadership style—not on someone else's. Once he was able to deal with his inner conflicts related to those issues, Mirabella's career proceeded without incident.

The Snare of Behaviorism

Even when coaches adopt a more empirically validated approach than McNulty did, they still tend to fall into the trap of treating the symptoms rather than the disorder. That's because they typically derive their treatments from behavioral psychology. Of course, behaviorism has been a great boon to psychiatry in recent years. Findings from this discipline have helped people enormously in controlling specific behaviors and learning to cope in particular situations. But treatments derived from behavioral psychology are sometimes too limited to address the problems that disrupt executives' ability to function.

One of the most popular behaviorist solutions is assertiveness training. This technique is most often used to help individuals cope with situations that evoke intense negative feelings—for example, helping drug addicts to "just say no" to temptation. Executive coaches use assertiveness training in a number of contexts. For instance, many coaches working with executives who appear to be lacking confidence employ the technique in an effort to get them to perform better. Unfortunately, learning effective responses to stressors often fails to help corporate executives deal with their intrapsychic pressures.

Take Jennifer Mansfield, vice president of training and development at a large software manufacturer. An acknowledged workaholic, Mansfield had followed a traditional path within her corporation, rising through the ranks by fulfilling every assignment with stellar results. When she was promoted to a managerial position, however, Mansfield's self-confidence began to slip. As a boss, she found it hard to delegate. Accustomed to delivering 110%, she was loath to cede control to her direct reports. She also found it impossible to give negative feedback. As a consequence, her work and that of her subordinates started to suffer, and she was missing deadlines.

Her boss presumed Mansfield was having an assertiveness problem, so he hired a coach from a consulting firm that specialized in behavioral treatments to work with her. The coach assumed that Mansfield needed to learn to set limits, to constructively criticize her subordinates, and to avoid the trap of doing other people's work for them. Within two months of what her coach deemed successful training, Mansfield began to lose weight, grow irritable, and display signs of exhaustion. At the time, I happened to be coaching the software company's COO, and he asked me to talk to her. It didn't take long to see how assertiveness training had unearthed a problem Mansfield had managed to keep under wraps for years.

Companies have a very tough time dealing with workaholics like Mansfield. Such individuals tend to sacrifice social and avocational pursuits in favor of work, and businesses value their productivity. It's hard to realize that these people have struck a Faustian bargain: trading success for "a life." Mansfield became a workaholic because she harbored a tremendous fear of intimacy. Although she was young, attractive, and likable, her parents' divorce and her mother's subsequent emotional suffering (communicated to Mansfield as "all men are bastards") left her fearful of forming intimate relationships with men. Those were easy for her to avoid when she managed discrete projects by putting in 80-hour work-weeks. But Mansfield could no longer do so when she became the manager of 11 professionals, seven of whom were men. For the first time in her career, males were showering her with attention, and the consequences were extremely disruptive.

Many coaches gain a Svengali-like hold over both the executives they train and the CEOs they report to, sometimes with disastrous consequences.

Mansfield could neither comprehend nor cope with the attention she received once promoted to the role of boss. While most managers would view the schmoozing and lobbying for attention that her reports engaged in as office politics, Mansfield saw these attempts at currying favor as trial balloons that might lead to dating. She was not being sexually harassed; Mansfield was merely experiencing interpersonal advances that threatened the protective fortress she had erected against feelings of intimacy. The better Mansfield managed the men in her division—and the more her constructive feedback improved their work—the more intimate they appeared to become as a natural outcome of their appreciation.

I passed this diagnosis along to the executive vice president of human resources, and he concurred. Mansfield's coaching ceased, and after her boss and I conducted a carefully crafted intervention, she agreed to seek outpatient psychotherapy. Several years later, Mansfield was thriving as a manager, and she had developed a more fulfilling personal life.

Not all executive coaches are as indifferent as Mansfield's was to underlying psychological disturbances. But those oversights are common when coaches focus on problems rather than people. Such coaches tend to define the problems plaguing an executive in the terms they understand best. If all you have is a hammer, everything looks like a nail.

The Trap of Influence

Executive coaches are at their most dangerous when they win the CEO's ear. This puts them in a position to wield great power over an entire organization, a scenario that occurs with disturbing frequency. Since many executive coaches were corporate types in prior lives, they connect with CEOs far more readily than most psychotherapists do. They are fluent in business patois, and they move easily from discussions of improving an individual's performance to conducting interventions that can help entire business units capture or retain market share. Unless these executive coaches have been trained in the dynamics of interpersonal relations, however, they may abuse their power—often without meaning to. Indeed, many coaches gain a Svengali-like hold over both the executives they train and the CEOs they report to, sometimes with disastrous consequences.

Take Rich Garvin, the CEO of an athletic shoe manufacturing company with sales in excess of $100 million a year. Despite his company's size, Garvin had never hired a coach for any of his direct reports. He knew that his HR director used trainers and coaches, but Garvin was a finance guy first and foremost. And since the athletic shoe industry was flying high, he left personnel matters to those who were paid to worry about them. But in the late 1990s, the market for athletic shoes collapsed. In Garvin's world, the most immediate casualty was his COO, who snapped under the strain of failing to meet sales estimates for three consecutive quarters. The COO began venting his frustration on store managers, buyers, and suppliers.

Garvin was under the gun during this difficult time, so he skipped the usual steps and sought the services of an executive coach on his own. He picked someone he knew well: Karl Nelson, whom Garvin had worked with at a major consulting firm when they were both starting their careers as freshly minted MBAs. Garvin thought he could trust Nelson to help manage his COO's anger and to mentor him through the storm. He also liked the sound of Nelson's coaching approach. It was based on a profiling system that diagnosed managers' strengths and weaknesses and charted career tracks that would optimize individual managers' productivity. This system was similar to the Myers-Briggs inventory, with many of psychologist Abraham Maslow's self-actualization principles thrown in. Garvin believed that Nelson and his system could help the COO.

Within six months of taking the assignment, Nelson claimed that the once-raging COO was calm and capable of fulfilling his duties. While this successful outcome was aided in large part by the athletic shoe industry's recovery, Garvin was nevertheless impressed with his friend's accomplishments. When Nelson suggested that he apply the profiling system to all the company's key executives, Garvin didn't give it a second thought.

During the next year, Nelson suggested a number of personnel changes. Since those came with the CEO's backing, the HR director accepted them, no questions asked. Because she was afraid to buck the CEO's hand-picked adviser, the personnel director also said nothing about the problems that ensued. These stemmed from Nelson's exclusive reliance on his profiling system. For example, in recommending the promotion of one East Coast store manager to regional director of West Coast sales, Nelson ignored the man's unfamiliarity with the region and the people he was appointed to manage. Not surprisingly, that move—and many of Nelson's other ill-conceived selections—bombed. To compound the problem, word of Nelson's status and his often horrific recommendations circulated through the company like wildfire, leading many people to both fear and resent his undue influence over Garvin. The negative emotions Nelson generated were so intense that underperforming, newly promoted managers became the targets of an undeclared, but uniformly embraced, pattern of passive-aggressive behavior by the rank and file. Such behaviors ranged from not attending meetings to botching orders to failing to stock goods in a timely manner.

Psychiatrists who've studied the Vietnam War are all too familiar with this type of hostile reaction to ineffectual leaders. Lieutenants fresh from ROTC training were hazed, sometimes even killed, by veteran troops who resented what they perceived to be an illegitimate attempt by the "F—ing New Guy" (FNG) to exercise authority. Military psychiatrists soon realized that these FNG lieutenants, clueless about the laws that governed life on the front lines, had been pulling rank in an effort to assert authority. The troopers did not take this well. In their view, the new lieutenants did not stack up to their predecessors, who had learned to let their hair down. To address the FNG syndrome, the military cautioned lieutenants to take it easy until the troopers accepted that they had developed field credentials.

When Garvin was confronted by a second decline in sales, this one precipitated by the FNG syndrome, he had no idea that Nelson's activities had caused the problem. In fact, because he believed that Nelson was expert in all matters of personnel functioning and efficiency, Garvin *increased* his reliance on his friend's counsel. He had become a victim of what, in the language of psychiatry, is called "transference"—a dynamic that gave Nelson extraordinary psychological power over Garvin.

Most people understand transference as "falling in love" with one's therapist. While this can be a manifestation, it paints an incomplete picture of the phenomenon. Transference can be positive or negative. Essentially, it is a powerful feeling for someone whose traits mirror those of a significant person—typically a parent—from one's past. Garvin formed a positive transference toward Nelson (who "saved" his COO). That placed Garvin in the role of an information-dependent child vis-à-vis an expert parent. Garvin relied on his coach to come up with best practices for handling problem executives. CEOs often form these sorts of relationships with their coaches.

Not all CEOs experience transference. Even so, coaches can easily expand their influence—from training to all-purpose advising—because CEOs don't like to lose face. Company leaders understand what coaches do and often feel personally responsible for selecting them. As a result, they feel more accountable for their coaches' successes or failures than they would if a psychotherapist were assigned to the case. In the same vein, when the CEO personally endorses a business plan, a number of psychological factors conspire to make it difficult to abandon that plan. Garvin was confronted with that situation when he authorized systemwide use of Nelson's personnel development procedures.

Garvin's story had a happy ending. Eventually he was persuaded to bring in a consulting firm to address the problems besetting his company. On the consultants' recommendation, he terminated Nelson's contract, and the FNG syndrome ceased. Not all CEOs are that lucky.

The Importance of Expertise

To best help their executives, companies need to draw on the expertise of both psychotherapists and executive coaches with legitimate skills. At a minimum, every executive slated to receive coaching should first receive a psychological evaluation. By screening out employees not psychologically prepared or predisposed to benefit from the process, companies avoid putting executives in deeply uncomfortable—even damaging—positions. Equally important, companies should hire independent mental health professionals to review coaching outcomes. This helps to ensure that coaches are not ignoring underlying problems or creating new ones, as Nelson did.

Psychological assessment and treatment are no silver bullet—and can in fact be gratuitous. For instance, a coach who trains executives to enhance their strategic-planning abilities need not be a psychiatrist. But don't assume that all executives who have planning problems lack the necessary skills. Can a psychological disorder interfere with developing a business plan? Absolutely, if the client suffers from clinical depression, which is known to block one's ability to engage in constructive, goal-oriented behavior. Without safeguards to prevent coaches from training those whose problems stem not from a lack of skills but from psychological problems, the executives being coached and the companies they work for will suffer.

The Economics of Executive Coaching

EXECUTIVE COACHING IS a major growth industry. At least 10,000 coaches work for businesses today, up from 2,000 in 1996. And that figure is expected to exceed 50,000 in the next five years. Executive coaching is also highly profitable; employers are now willing to pay fees ranging from $1,500 to $15,000 a day. That's a lot more than any psychotherapist could even dream of charging. Why are companies willing to pay so much more for their coaches?

The answer is simple: Executive coaches offer seemingly quick and easy solutions. CEOs tell me that what they fear most about psychotherapy is not the cost in dollars but the cost in time. A coaching engagement typically lasts no more then six months. Psychotherapy, by contrast, is seen as long-term treatment; people joke that it takes six moths for a therapist and patient just to say hello. What's more, therapy requires a greater time commitment than the standard 50-minute sessions; it also involves travel to and from the therapist's office, taking even more time away from work.

If coaching fails to cure a problem in six months, it can become very expensive indeed. Take the case of Tom Davis, the coach who worked with Rob Bernstein, the executive VP of sales at an automotive parts distributor. Let's assume Davis charged a relatively low per diem of $1,500. Over the four years of his engagement—which ultimately did not solve Bernstein's problems—he would have picked up at least $45,000 in fees. That sum would have purchased 450 hours with a competent therapist—about ten years' worth of weekly sessions.

Originally published in June 2002
Reprint R0206E

Narcissistic Leaders

The Incredible Pros, the Inevitable Cons

MICHAEL MACCOBY

Executive Summary

TODAY'S BUSINESS LEADERS maintain a markedly higher profile than their predecessors did in the 1950s through the 1980s. Rather then hide behind the corporate veil, they give interviews to magazines like *Business Week, Time,* and the *Economist.* According to psychoanalyst, anthropologist, and consultant Michael Maccoby, this love of the limelight often stems from their personalities—in particular, what Freud called a narcissistic personality.

That is both good and bad news: Narcissists are good for companies that need people with vision and the courage to take them in new directions. But narcissists can also lead companies into trouble by refusing to listen to the advice and warnings of their managers.

So what can the narcissistic leader do to avoid the traps of his own personality? First, he can find a trusted sidekick. Good sidekicks can point out the operational requirements of the narcissistic leader's often grandiose vision and keep him rooted in reality. Second, the narcissistic leader can get the people in his organization to identify with his goals, to think the way he does, and to become the living embodiment of the company. Finally, if narcissistic leaders can be persuaded to undergo therapy, they can use tools such as psychoanalysis to help overcome vital character flaws.

With the dramatic discontinuities going on in the world today, more and more larger corporations are finding there is no substitute for narcissistic leaders. For companies whose narcissistic leaders recognize their limits, these will be the best of times. For other companies, these could be the worst.

THERE'S SOMETHING NEW AND DARING about the CEOs who are transforming today's industries. Just compare them with the executives who ran large companies in the 1950s through the 1980s. Those executives shunned the press and had their comments carefully crafted by corporate PR departments. But today's CEOs—superstars such as Bill Gates, Andy Grove, Steve Jobs, Jeff Bezos, and Jack Welch—hire their own publicists, write books, grant spontaneous interviews, and actively promote their personal philosophies. Their faces adorn the covers of magazines like *Business Week*, *Time*, and the *Economist*. What's more, the world's business personalities are increasingly seen as the makers and shapers of our public and personal agendas. They advise schools on what kids should learn and lawmakers on how to invest the public's money. We look to them for thoughts on everything from the future of e-commerce to hot places to vacation.

There are many reasons today's business leaders have higher profiles than ever before. One is that business plays a much bigger role in our lives than it used to, and its leaders are more often in the limelight. Another is that the business world is experiencing enormous changes that call for visionary and charismatic leadership. But my 25 years of consulting both as a psychoanalyst in private practice and as an adviser to top managers suggest a third reason—namely, a pronounced change in the personality of the strategic leaders at the top. As an anthropologist, I try to understand people in the context in which they operate, and as a psychoanalyst, I tend to see them through a distinctly Freudian lens. Given what I know, I believe that the larger-than-life leaders we are seeing today closely resemble the personality type that Sigmund Freud dubbed narcissistic. "People of this type impress others as being 'personalities,'" he wrote, describing one of the psychological types that clearly fall within the range of normality. "They are especially suited to act as a support for others, to take on the role of leaders, and to give a fresh stimulus to cultural development or damage the established state of affairs."

Throughout history, narcissists have always emerged to inspire people and to shape the future. When military, religious, and political arenas dominated society, it was figures such as Napoléon Bonaparte, Mahatma Gandhi, and Franklin Delano Roosevelt who determined the social agenda. But from time to time, when business became the engine of social change, it, too, generated its share of narcissistic leaders. That was true at the

beginning of this century, when men like Andrew
Carnegie, John D. Rockefeller, Thomas Edison, and
Henry Ford exploited new technologies and restructured
American industry. And I think it is true again today.

But Freud recognized that there is a dark side to narcissism. Narcissists, he pointed out, are emotionally isolated and highly distrustful. Perceived threats can trigger
rage. Achievements can feed feelings of grandiosity.

Productive narcissists have the audacity to push through the massive transformations that society periodically undertakes.

That's why Freud thought narcissists were the hardest personality types to analyze. Consider how an executive at Oracle describes his nar-
cissistic CEO Larry Elli-
son: "The difference between God and Larry is that God
does not believe he is Larry." That observation is amus-
ing, but it is also troubling. Not surprisingly, most people
think of narcissists in a primarily negative way. After all,
Freud named the type after the mythical figure Narcis-
sus, who died because of his pathological preoccupation
with himself.

Yet narcissism can be extraordinarily useful—even
necessary. Freud shifted his views about narcissism over
time and recognized that we are all somewhat narcissistic. More recently, psychoanalyst Heinz Kohut built on
Freud's theories and developed methods of treating narcissists. Of course, only professional clinicians are trained
to tell if narcissism is normal or pathological. In this
article, I discuss the differences between productive and
unproductive narcissism but do not explore the extreme
pathology of borderline conditions and psychosis.

Leaders such as Jack Welch and George Soros are
examples of productive narcissists. They are gifted and

creative strategists who see the big picture and find meaning in the risky challenge of changing the world and leaving behind a legacy. Indeed, one reason we look to productive narcissists in times of great transition is that they have the audacity to push through the massive transformations that society periodically undertakes. Productive narcissists are not only risk takers willing to get the job done but also charmers who can convert the masses with their rhetoric. The danger is that narcissism can turn unproductive when, lacking self-knowledge and restraining anchors, narcissists become unrealistic dreamers. They nurture grand schemes and harbor the illusion that only circumstances or enemies block their success. This tendency toward grandiosity and distrust is the Achilles' heel of narcissists. Because of it, even brilliant narcissists can come under suspicion for self-involvement, unpredictability, and—in extreme cases— paranoia.

It's easy to see why narcissistic leadership doesn't always mean successful leadership. Consider the case of Volvo's Pehr Gyllenhammar. He had a dream that appealed to a broad international audience—a plan to revolutionize the industrial workplace by replacing the dehumanizing assembly line caricatured in Charlie Chaplin's *Modern Times*. His wildly popular vision called for team-based craftsmanship. Model factories were built and publicized to international acclaim. But his success in pushing through these dramatic changes also sowed the seeds for his downfall. Gyllenhammar started to feel that he could ignore the concerns of his operational managers. He pursued chancy and expensive business deals, which he publicized on television and in the press. On one level, you can ascribe Gyllenhammar's falling out of touch with his workforce simply to faulty

strategy. But it is also possible to attribute it to his narcissistic personality. His overestimation of himself led
him to believe that others would want him to be the czar
of a multinational enterprise. In turn, these fantasies led
him to pursue a merger with Renault, which was tremen-
dously unpopular with Swedish employees. Because Gyllenhammar was deaf to complaints about Renault,
Swedish managers were forced to take their case public.
In the end, shareholders aggressively rejected Gyllenhammar's plan, leaving him with no option but to resign.

Given the large number of narcissists at the helm of
corporations today, the challenge facing organizations is
to ensure that such leaders do not self-destruct or lead
the company to disaster. That can take some doing
because it is very hard for narcissists to work through
their issues—and virtually impossible for them to do it
alone. Narcissists need colleagues and even therapists if
they hope to break free from their limitations. But
because of their extreme independence and self-protec-
tiveness, it is very difficult to get near them. Kohut main-
tained that a therapist would have to demonstrate an
extraordinarily profound empathic understanding and
sympathy for the narcissist's feelings in order to gain his
trust. On top of that, narcissists must recognize that they
can benefit from such help. For their part, employees
must learn how to recognize—and work around—narcissistic bosses. To help them in this endeavor, let's first
take a closer look at Freud's theory of personality types.

Three Main Personality Types

While Freud recognized that there are an almost infinite
variety of personalities, he identified three main types:
erotic, obsessive, and narcissistic. Most of us have ele-
ments of all three. We are all, for example, somewhat

narcissistic. If that were not so, we would not be able to survive or assert our needs. The point is, one of the dynamic tendencies usually dominates the others, making each of us react differently to success and failure.

Freud's definitions of personality types differed over time. When talking about the erotic personality type, however, Freud generally did not mean a sexual personality but rather one for whom loving and above all being loved is most important. This type of individual is dependent on those people they fear will stop loving them. Many erotics are teachers, nurses, and social workers. At their most productive, they are developers of the young as well as enablers and helpers at work. As managers, they are caring and supportive, but they avoid conflict and make people dependent on them. They are, according to Freud, outer-directed people.

Obsessives, in contrast, are inner-directed. They are self-reliant and conscientious. They create and maintain order and make the most effective operational managers. They look constantly for ways to help people listen better, resolve conflict, and find win-win opportunities. They buy self-improvement books such as Stephen Covey's *The 7 Habits of Highly Effective People*. Obsessives are also ruled by a strict conscience—they like to focus on continuous improvement at work because it fits in with their sense of moral improvement. As entrepreneurs, obsessives start businesses that express their values, but they lack the vision, daring, and charisma it takes to turn a good idea into a great one. The best obsessives set high standards and communicate very effectively. They make sure that instructions are followed and costs are kept within budget. The most productive are great mentors and team players. The unproductive and the uncooperative become narrow experts and rule-bound bureaucrats.

Narcissists, the third type, are independent and not easily impressed. They are innovators, driven in business to gain power and glory. Productive narcissists are experts in their industries, but they go beyond it. They also pose the critical questions. They want to learn everything about everything that affects the company and its products. Unlike erotics, they want to be admired, not loved. And unlike obsessives, they are not troubled by a punishing superego, so they are able to aggressively pursue their goals. Of all the personality types, narcissists run the greatest risk of isolating themselves at the moment of success. And because of their independence and aggressiveness, they are constantly looking out for enemies, sometimes degenerating into paranoia when they are under extreme stress. (For more on personality types, see "Fromm's Fourth Personality Type" at the end of this article.)

Strengths of the Narcissistic Leader

When it comes to leadership, personality type can be instructive. Erotic personalities generally make poor managers—they need too much approval. Obsessives make better leaders—they are your operational managers: critical and cautious. But it is narcissists who come closest to our collective image of great leaders. There are two reasons for this: they have compelling, even gripping, visions for companies, and they have an ability to attract followers.

GREAT VISION

I once asked a group of managers to define a leader. "A person with vision" was a typical response. Productive narcissists understand the vision thing particularly well, because they are by nature people who see the big picture. They are not analyzers who can break up big questions into manageable problems; they aren't number crunchers either (these are usually the obsessives). Nor do they try to extrapolate to understand the future— they attempt to create it. To paraphrase George Bernard Shaw, some people see things as they are and ask why; narcissists see things that never were and ask why not.

Consider the difference between Bob Allen, a productive obsessive, and Mike Armstrong, a productive narcissist. In 1997, Allen tried to expand AT&T to reestablish the end-to-end service of the Bell System by reselling local service from the regional Bell operating companies (RBOCs). Although this was a worthwhile endeavor for shareholders and customers, it was hardly earth-shattering. By contrast, through a strategy of combining voice, telecommunications, and Internet access by high-speed broadband telecommunication over cable, Mike Armstrong has "created a new space with his name on it," as one of his colleagues puts it. Armstrong is betting that his costly strategy will beat out the RBOC's less expensive solution of digital subscriber lines over copper wire. This example illustrates the different approaches of obsessives and narcissists. The risk Armstrong took is one that few obsessives would feel comfortable taking. His vision is galvanizing AT&T. Who but a narcissistic leader could achieve such a thing? As Napoleon—a classic narcissist—once remarked, "Revolutions are ideal times for soldiers with a lot of wit—and the courage to act."

As in the days of the French Revolution, the world is now changing in astounding ways; narcissists have opportunities they would never have in ordinary times.

In short, today's narcissistic leaders have the chance to change the very rules of the game. Consider Robert B. Shapiro, CEO of Monsanto. Shapiro described his vision of genetically modifying crops as "the single most successful introduction of technology in the history of agriculture, including the plow" (*New York Times*, August 5, 1999). This is certainly a huge claim—there are still many questions about the safety and public acceptance of genetically engineered fruits and vegetables. But industries like agriculture are desperate for radical change. If Shapiro's gamble is successful, the industry will be transformed in the image of Monsanto. That's why he can get away with painting a picture of Monsanto as a highly profitable "life sciences" company—despite the fact that Monsanto's stock has fallen 12% from 1998 to the end of the third quarter of 1999. (During the same period, the S&P was up 41%.) Unlike Armstrong and Shapiro, it was enough for Bob Allen to win against his competitors in a game measured primarily by the stock market. But narcissistic leaders are after something more. They want—and need—to leave behind a legacy.

SCORES OF FOLLOWERS

Narcissists have vision—but that's not enough. People in mental hospitals also have visions. The simplest definition of a leader is someone whom other people follow. Indeed, narcissists are especially gifted in attracting followers, and more often than not, they do so through language. Narcissists believe that words can move mountains and that inspiring speeches can change people. Narcissistic leaders are often skillful orators, and this is one of the talents that makes them so charismatic.

Indeed, anyone who has seen narcissists perform can attest to their personal magnetism and their ability to stir enthusiasm among audiences.

Yet this charismatic gift is more of a two-way affair than most people think. Although it is not always obvious, narcissistic leaders are quite dependent on their followers—they need affirmation, and preferably adulation. Think of Winston Churchill's wartime broadcasts or J.F.K.'s "Ask not what your country can do for you" inaugural address. The adulation that follows from such speeches bolsters the self-confidence and conviction of the speakers. But if no one responds, the narcissist usually becomes insecure, overly shrill, and insistent—just as Ross Perot did.

Even when people respond positively to a narcissist, there are dangers. That's because charisma is a double-edged sword—it fosters both closeness and isolation. As he becomes increasingly self-assured, the narcissist becomes more spontaneous. He feels free of constraints. Ideas flow. He thinks he's invincible. This energy and confidence further inspire his followers. But the very adulation that the narcissist demands can have a corrosive effect. As he expands, he listens even less to words of caution and advice. After all, he has been right before, when others had their doubts. Rather than try to persuade those who disagree with him, he feels justified in ignoring them—creating further isolation. The result is sometimes flagrant risk taking that can lead to catastrophe. In the political realm, there is no clearer example of this than Bill Clinton.

One of his greatest problems is that the narcissist's faults tend to become even more pronounced as he becomes more successful.

Weaknesses of the Narcissistic Leader

Despite the warm feelings their charisma can evoke, narcissists are typically not comfortable with their own emotions. They listen only for the kind of information they seek. They don't learn easily from others. They don't like to teach but prefer to indoctrinate and make speeches. They dominate meetings with subordinates. The result for the organization is greater internal competitiveness at a time when everyone is already under as much pressure as they can possibly stand. Perhaps the main problem is that the narcissist's faults tend to become even more pronounced as he becomes more successful.

SENSITIVE TO CRITICISM

Because they are extraordinarily sensitive, narcissistic leaders shun emotions as a whole. Indeed, perhaps one of the greatest paradoxes in this age of teamwork and partnering is that the best corporate leader in the contemporary world is the type of person who is emotionally isolated. Narcissistic leaders typically keep others at arm's length. They can put up a wall of defense as thick as the Pentagon. And given their difficulty with knowing or acknowledging their own feelings, they are uncomfortable with other people expressing theirs—especially their negative feelings.

Indeed, even productive narcissists are extremely sensitive to criticism or slights, which feel to them like knives threatening their self-image and their confidence in their visions. Narcissists are almost unimaginably thin-skinned. Like the fairy-tale princess who slept on many mattresses and yet knew she was sleeping on a pea, narcissists—even powerful CEOs—bruise easily. This is one explanation why narcissistic leaders do not want to know what people think of them unless it is causing them a real problem. They cannot tolerate dissent. In fact, they can be extremely abrasive with employees who doubt them or with subordinates who are tough enough to fight back. Steve Jobs, for example, publicly humiliates subordinates. Thus, although narcissistic leaders often say that they want teamwork, what that means in practice is that they want a group of yes-men. As the more independent-minded players leave or are pushed out, succession becomes a particular problem.

POOR LISTENERS

One serious consequence of this oversensitivity to criticism is that narcissistic leaders often do not listen when they feel threatened or attacked. Consider the response of one narcissistic CEO I had worked with for three years who asked me to interview his immediate team and report back to him on what they were thinking. He invited me to his summer home to discuss what I had found. "So what do they think of me?" he asked with seeming nonchalance. "They think you are very creative and courageous," I told him, "but they also feel that you don't listen." "Excuse me, what did you say?" he shot back at once, pretending not to hear. His response was humorous, but it was also tragic. In a very real way, this CEO could not hear my criticism because it was too painful to tolerate. Some narcissists are so defensive that they go so far as to make a virtue of the fact that they don't listen. As another CEO bluntly put it, "I didn't get here by listening to people!" Indeed, on one occasion when this CEO proposed a daring strategy, none of his subordinates believed it would work. His subsequent success strengthened his conviction that he had nothing to learn about strategy from his lieutenants. But success is no excuse for narcissistic leaders not to listen.

LACK OF EMPATHY

Best-selling business writers today have taken up the slogan of "emotional competencies"—the belief that successful leadership requires a strongly developed sense of empathy. But although they crave empathy from others, productive narcissists are not noted for being particularly empathetic themselves. Indeed, lack of empathy is a characteristic shortcoming of some of the most charismatic and successful narcissists, including Bill Gates and Andy Grove. Of course, leaders do need to communicate persuasively. But a lack of empathy did not prevent some of history's greatest narcissistic leaders from knowing how to communicate—and inspire. Neither Churchill, de Gaulle, Stalin, nor Mao Tse-tung were empathetic. And yet they inspired people because of their passion and their conviction at a time when people longed for certainty. In fact, in times of radical change, lack of empathy can actually be a strength. A narcissist finds it easier than other personality types to buy and sell companies, to close and move facilities, and to lay off employees—decisions that inevitably make many people angry and sad. But narcissistic leaders typically have few regrets. As one

There is a kind of emotional intelligence associated with narcissists, but it's more street smarts than empathy.

CEO says," If I listened to my employees' needs and demands, they would eat me alive."

Given this lack of empathy, it's hardly surprising that narcissistic leaders don't score particularly well on evaluations of their interpersonal style. What's more, neither 360-degree evaluations of their management style nor workshops in listening will make them more empathic. Narcissists don't want to change—and as long as they are successful, they don't think they have to. They may see the need for operational managers to get touchy-feely training, but that's not for them.

There is a kind of emotional intelligence associated with narcissists, but it's more street smarts than empathy. Narcissistic leaders are acutely aware of whether or not people are with them wholeheartedly. They know whom they can use. They can be brutally exploitative. That's why, even though narcissists undoubtedly have "star quality," they are often unlikable. They easily stir up people against them, and it is only in tumultuous times, when their gifts are desperately needed, that people are willing to tolerate narcissists as leaders.

DISTASTE FOR MENTORING

Lack of empathy and extreme independence make it difficult for narcissists to mentor and be mentored. Generally speaking, narcissistic leaders set very little store by mentoring. They seldom mentor others, and when they do they typically want their protégés to be pale reflections of themselves. Even those narcissists like Jack Welch who are held up as strong mentors are usually more interested in instructing than in coaching.

Narcissists certainly don't credit mentoring or educational programs for their own development as leaders. A few narcissistic leaders such as Bill Gates may find a friend or consultant—for instance, Warren Buffett, a superproductive obsessive—whom they can trust to be their guide and confidant. But most narcissists prefer "mentors" they can control. A 32-year-old marketing vice president, a narcissist with CEO potential, told me that she had rejected her boss as a mentor. As she put it, "First of all, I want to keep the relationship at a distance. I don't want to be influenced by emotions. Second, there are things I don't want him to know. I'd rather hire an outside consultant to be my coach." Although narcissistic leaders appear to be at ease with others, they find intimacy—which is a prerequisite for mentoring—to be difficult. Younger narcissists will establish peer relations with authority rather than seek a parentlike mentoring relationship. They want results and are willing to take chances arguing with authority.

AN INTENSE DESIRE TO COMPETE

Narcissistic leaders are relentless and ruthless in their pursuit of victory. Games are not games but tests of their survival skills. Of course, all successful managers want to win, but narcissists are not restrained by conscience. Organizations led by narcissists are generally characterized by intense internal competition. Their passion to win is marked by both the promise of glory and the primitive danger of extinction. It is a potent brew that energizes companies, creating a sense of urgency, but it can also be dangerous. These leaders see everything as a threat. As Andy Grove puts it, brilliantly articulating the narcissist's fear, distrust, and aggression, "Only the paranoid survive." The concern, of course, is that the narcissist finds enemies that aren't there—even among his colleagues.

Avoiding the Traps

There is very little business literature that tells narcissistic leaders how to avoid the pitfalls. There are two reasons for this. First, relatively few narcissistic leaders are interested in looking inward. And second, psychoanalysts don't usually get close enough to them, especially in the workplace, to write about them. (The noted psychoanalyst Harry Levinson is an exception.) As a result, advice on leadership focuses on obsessives, which explains why so much of it is about creating teamwork and being more receptive to subordinates. But as we've already seen, this literature is of little interest to narcissists, nor is it likely to help subordinates understand their narcissistic leaders. The absence of managerial literature on narcissistic leaders doesn't mean that it is impossible to devise strategies for dealing with narcissism. In the course of a long career counseling CEOs, I have identified three basic ways in which productive narcissists can avoid the traps of their own personality.

FIND A TRUSTED SIDEKICK

Many narcissists can develop a close relationship with one person, a sidekick who acts as an anchor, keeping the narcissistic partner grounded. However, given that narcissistic leaders trust only their own insights and view of reality, the sidekick has to understand the narcissistic leader and what he is trying to achieve. The narcissist must feel that this person, or in some cases

persons, is practically an extension of himself. The sidekick must also be sensitive enough to manage the
relationship. Don Quixote is a classic example of a narcissist who was out of touch with reality but who was
constantly saved from disaster by his squire Sancho
Panza. Not surprisingly, many narcissistic leaders rely
heavily on their spouses, the people they are closest to.
But dependence on spouses can be risky, because they
may further isolate the narcissistic leader from his company by supporting his grandiosity and feeding his
paranoia. I once knew a CEO in this kind of relationship with his spouse. He took to accusing loyal subordinates of plotting against him just because they
ventured a few criticisms of his ideas.

It is much better for a narcissistic leader to choose a
colleague as his sidekick. Good sidekicks are able to
point out the operational requirements of the narcissistic leader's vision and keep him rooted in reality. The
best sidekicks are usually productive obsessives. Gyllenhammar, for instance, was most effective at Volvo when
he had an obsessive COO, Håkan Frisinger, to focus on
improving quality and cost, as well as an obsessive HR
director, Berth Jönsson, to implement his vision. Similarly, Bill Gates can think about the future from the
stratosphere because Steve Ballmer, a tough obsessive
president, keeps the show on the road. At Oracle, CEO
Larry Ellison can afford to miss key meetings and spend
time on his boat contemplating a future without PCs
because he has a productive obsessive COO in Ray Lane
to run the company for him. But the job of sidekick
entails more than just executing the leader's ideas. The
sidekick also has to get his leader to accept new ideas. To
do this, he must be able to show the leader how the new
ideas fit with his views and serve his interests. (For more

on dealing with narcissistic bosses, see "Working for a
Narcissist" at the end of this article.)

INDOCTRINATE THE ORGANIZATION

The narcissistic CEO wants all his subordinates to think
the way he does about the business. Productive narcissists—people who often have a dash of the obsessive personality—are good at converting people to their point of
view. One of the most successful at this is GE's Jack
Welch. Welch uses toughness to build a corporate culture and to implement a daring business strategy,
including the buying and selling of scores of companies.
Unlike other narcissistic leaders such as Gates, Grove,
and Ellison, who have transformed industries with new
products, Welch was able to transform his industry by
focusing on execution and pushing companies to the
limits of quality and efficiency, bumping up revenues and
wringing out costs. In order to do so, Welch hammers
out a huge corporate culture in his own image—a culture
that provides impressive rewards for senior managers
and shareholders.

Welch's approach to culture building is widely mis-
understood. Many observers, notably Noel Tichy in *The
Leadership Engine*, argue that Welch forms his company's leadership culture through teaching. But Welch's
"teaching" involves a personal ideology that he indoctri-
nates into GE managers through speeches, memos, and
confrontations. Rather than create a dialogue, Welch
makes pronouncements (either be the number one or
two company in your market or get out), and he insti-
tutes programs (such as Six Sigma quality) that become
the GE party line. Welch's strategy has been extremely
effective. GE managers must either internalize his

vision, or they must leave. Clearly, this is incentive learning with a vengeance. I would even go so far as to call Welch's teaching brainwashing. But Welch does have the rare insight and know-how to achieve what all narcissistic business leaders are trying to do—namely, get the organization to identify with them, to think the way they do, and to become the living embodiment of their companies.

GET INTO ANALYSIS

Narcissists are often more interested in controlling others than in knowing and disciplining themselves. That's why, with very few exceptions, even productive narcissists do not want to explore their personalities with the help of insight therapies such as psychoanalysis. Yet since Heinz Kohut, there has been a radical shift in psychoanalytic thinking about what can be done to help narcissists work through their rage, alienation, and grandiosity. Indeed, if they can be persuaded to undergo therapy, narcissistic leaders can use tools such as psychoanalysis to overcome vital character flaws.

Consider the case of one exceptional narcissistic CEO who asked me to help him understand why he so often lost his temper with subordinates. He lived far from my home city, and so the therapy was sporadic and very unorthodox. Yet he kept a journal of his dreams, which we interpreted together either by phone or when we met. Our analysis uncovered painful feelings of being unappreciated that went back to his inability to impress a cold father. He came to realize that he demanded an unreasonable amount of praise and that when he felt unappreciated by his subordinates, he became furious. Once he understood that, he was able to recognize his narcissism and even laugh about it. In the middle of our work, he even announced to his top team that I was psychoanalyzing him and asked them what they thought of that. After a pregnant pause, one executive vice president piped up, "Whatever you're doing, you should keep doing it, because you don't get so angry anymore." Instead of being trapped by narcissistic rage, this CEO was learning how to express his concerns constructively.

Leaders who can work on themselves in that way tend to be the most productive narcissists. In addition to being self-reflective, they are also likely to be open, likable, and good-humored. Productive narcissists have perspective; they are able to detach themselves and laugh at their irrational needs. Although serious about achieving their goals, they are also playful. As leaders, they are aware of being performers. A sense of humor helps them maintain enough perspective and humility to keep on learning.

The Best and Worst of Times

As I have pointed out, narcissists thrive in chaotic times. In more tranquil times and places, however, even the most brilliant narcissist will seem out of place. In his short story *The Curfew Tolls*, Stephen Vincent Benét speculates on what would have happened to Napoléon if he had been born some 30 years earlier. Retired in prerevolutionary France, Napoléon is depicted as a lonely artillery major boasting to a vacationing British general about how he could have beaten the English in India. The point, of course, is that a visionary born in the wrong time can seem like a pompous buffoon.

Historically, narcissists in large corporations have been confined to sales positions, where they use their persuasiveness and imagination to best effect. In settled times, the problematic side of the narcissistic personality usually conspires to keep narcissists in their place, and

More and more corporations are finding there is no substitute for narcissistic leaders in this age of innovation.

they can typically rise to top management positions only by starting their own companies or by leaving to lead upstarts. Consider Joe Nacchio, formerly in charge of both the business

and consumer divisions of AT&T. Nacchio was a super-salesman and a popular leader in the mid-1990s. But his desire to create a new network for business customers was thwarted by colleagues who found him abrasive, self-promoting, and ruthlessly ambitious.

Two years ago, Nacchio left AT&T to become CEO of Qwest, a company that is creating a long-distance fiber-optic cable network. Nacchio had the credibility—and charisma—to sell Qwest's initial public offering to financial markets and gain a high valuation. Within a short space of time, he turned Qwest into an attractive target for the RBOCs, which were looking to move into long-distance telephony and Internet services. Such a sale would have given Qwest's owners a handsome profit on their investment. But Nacchio wanted more. He wanted to expand—to compete with AT&T—and for that he needed local service. Rather than sell Qwest, he chose to make a bid himself for local telephone operator U.S. West, using Qwest's highly valued stock to finance the deal. The market voted on this display of expansiveness with its feet—Qwest's stock price fell 40% between last June, when he made the deal, and the end of the third quarter of 1999. (The S&P index dropped 5.7% during the same period.)

Like other narcissists, Nacchio likes risk—and sometimes ignores the costs. But with the dramatic discontinuities going on in the world today, more and more large
corporations are getting into bed with narcissists. They
are finding that there is no substitute for narcissistic leaders in an age of innovation. Companies need leaders who
do not try to anticipate the future so much as create it.
But narcissistic leaders—even the most productive of
them—can self-destruct and lead their organizations ter-
ribly astray. For companies whose narcissistic leaders recognize their limitations, these will be the best of times.
For other companies, these could turn out to be the worst.

Fromm's Fourth Personality Type

NOT LONG AFTER FREUD described his three personality types in 1931, psychoanalyst Erich Fromm proposed
a fourth personality type, which has become particularly
prevalent in today's service economy. Fromm called this
type the "marketing personality," and it is exemplified by
the lead character in Woody Allen's movie *Zelig*, a man
so governed by his need to be valued that he becomes
exactly like the people he happens to be around.

Marketing personalities are more detached than
erotics and so are less likely to cement close ties. They
are also less driven by conscience than obsessives.
Instead, they are motivated by a radarlike anxiety that
permeates everything they do. Because they are so
eager to please and to alleviate this anxiety, marketing
personalities excel at selling themselves to others.

Unproductive marketing types lack direction and the
ability to commit themselves to people or projects. But

when productive, marketing types are good at facilitating teams and keeping the focus on adding value as defined by customers and colleagues. Like obsessives, marketing personalities are avid consumers of self-help books. Like narcissists, they are not wedded to the past. But marketing types generally make poor leaders in times of crisis. They lack the daring needed to innovate and are too responsive to current, rather than future, customer demands.

The Rise and Fall of a Narcissist

THE STORY OF JAN CARLZON, the former CEO of the Scandinavian airline SAS, is an almost textbook example of how a narcissist's weaknesses can cut short a brilliant career. In the 1980s, Carlzon's vision of SAS as the businessperson's airline was widely acclaimed in the business press; management guru Tom Peters described him as a model leader. In 1989, when I first met Carlzon and his management team, he compared the ideal organization to the Brazilian soccer team—in principle, there would be no fixed roles, only innovative plays. I asked the members of the management team if they agreed with this vision of an empowered front line. One vice president, a former pilot, answered no. "I still believe that the best organization is the military," he said. I then asked Carlzon for his reaction to that remark. "Well," he replied, "that may be true, if your goal is to shoot your customers."

That rejoinder was both witty and dismissive; clearly, Carlzon was not engaging in a serious dialogue with his subordinates. Nor was he listening to other advisers.

Carlzon ignored the issue of high costs, even when many observers pointed out that SAS could not compete without improving productivity. He threw money at expensive acquisitions of hotels and made an unnecessary investment in Continental Airlines just months before it declared bankruptcy.

Carlzon's story perfectly corroborates the often-recorded tendency of narcissists to become overly expansive—and hence isolated—at the very pinnacle of their success. Seduced by the flattery he received in the international press, Carlzon's self-image became so enormously inflated that his feet left the ground. And given his vulnerability to grandiosity, he was propelled by a need to expand his organization rather than develop it. In due course, as Carlzon led the company deeper and deeper into losses, he was fired. Now he is a venture capitalist helping budding companies. And SAS has lost its glitter.

Working for a Narcissist

DEALING WITH A narcissistic boss isn't easy. You have to be prepared to look for another job if your boss becomes too narcissistic to let you disagree with him. But remember that the company is typically betting on *his* vision of the future—not yours. Here are a few tips on how to survive in the short term:

- Always empathize with your boss's feelings, but don't expect any empathy back. Look elsewhere for your own self-esteem. Understand that behind his display of infallibility, there hides a deep vulnerability. Praise his achievements and reinforce his best impulses, but don't be shamelessly sycophantic. An intelligent narcissist can see through flatterers and prefers independent people who truly appreciate him. Show that you will protect his image, inside and outside the company. But be careful if he asks for an honest evaluation. What he wants is information that will help him solve a problem about his image. He will resent any honesty that threatens his inflated self-image and will likely retaliate.

- Give your boss ideas, but always let him take the credit for them. Find out what he thinks before presenting your views. If you believe he is wrong, show how a different approach would be in his best interest. Take his paranoid views seriously, don't brush them aside—they often reveal sharp intuitions. Disagree only when you can demonstrate how he will benefit from a different point of view.

- Hone your time-management skills. Narcissistic leaders often give subordinates many more orders than they can possibly execute. Ignore the requests he makes that don't make sense. Forget about them. He will. But be careful: carve out free time for yourself only when you know there's a lull in the boss's schedule. Narcissistic leaders feel free to call you at any hour of the day or night. Make yourself available, or be prepared to get out.

Originally published in January–February 2000
Reprint R00105

The Leadership Journey

LEONARD D. SCHAEFFER

Executive Summary

IT ISN'T ALWAYS EASY TO change leadership hats or
to alter the way you assess a business problem. Under
pressure, most executives fall back on the management
style or approach that worked in the last crisis they
faced. But old approaches rarely work in new and
demanding situations.

Just ask Leonard Schaeffer, chairman and CEO of
WellPoint Health Networks, one of the country's largest
and most successful managed-care companies. In this
account, he describes how he consciously adopted
three very different styles of leadership at critical points
during his 30-year career, depending on the business
challenges at hand.

Schaeffer headed up the U.S. Health Care Finance
Administration during the Carter years—and led the
charge toward more efficient work practices at that

agency. Then he transformed Blue Cross of California from a floundering bureaucracy losing close to $1 million each day into a strong public company, WellPoint. The dire circumstances at Blue Cross had dictated that Schaeffer initially be an autocratic leader, which he considers the managerial equivalent of being an emergency room surgeon—forced to do whatever it takes to save a patient's life. But as the company rebounded, the CEO shed that "any decision is better than no decision" style. He has become a participative, hands-off leader—setting strategies and goals from above but letting WellPoint's line managers and executives figure out how best to achieve those goals. Most recently, Schaeffer has turned into a reformer—a leader who works with one foot outside the company to spur changes in health care and society.

There are pitfalls in switching leadership styles, Schaeffer admits, but this flexibility is necessary for realizing corporate—and personal—success.

Monday, february 10, 1986 was my first day as chief executive of Blue Cross of California. At a welcoming reception, the company presented me with a sculpture, nearly five feet tall, of a cross carved from blue ice and artistically decorated with succulent pink prawns. The thing was exquisitely beautiful—and the most apt emblem for wasteful spending I'd ever seen. When I asked where it came from, I was introduced to the company's pastry chef. My first official act was to fire him. After all, Blue Cross of California was at that time the worst-performing of the 77 Blue Cross plans across the country, with annual operating losses of $165 million. With the organization teetering on the edge of insolvency, ice sculpting hardly seemed like a core function.

Sixteen years have passed since I let that pastry chef go. In that time, Blue Cross of California has transformed itself from a floundering bureaucracy into a strong public company called WellPoint Health Networks, one of the largest health insurance organizations in the United States. The company now serves more than 45 million people nationwide through pharmacy benefits, dental plans, mental health plans, PPOs, and HMOs. Better yet, we've grown from revenues of $2 billion in 1987 to $16 billion today. We've been consistently profitable since 1989.

As the company has changed, I've gone through my own transformation as chief executive. The top-down, autocratic style I had to adopt to turn around the business gave way to a more hands-off style that focused on motivating others to act rather than managing them directly. And more recently, I've been going through yet another shift—away from the participative mode and toward what I call a reformer style of leadership in which the chief executive's role is to represent the company's interests on a broader stage. This style of leadership requires interacting more with customers, elected officials, and other industry executives to help spur fundamental changes in an industry and even in society.

An autocratic leader is the managerial equivalent of an emergency room surgeon, forced to do whatever it takes to save a patient's life.

Over the course of my 30-year career, I've come to understand that leadership is about more than heavy-handed action from the top. Its defining characteristics change according to the needs and vagaries of the individual, the organization, the industry, and the world at large. In other words, leadership is not a state, it's a journey. There aren't always sharp dividing lines between one style of leadership and another—an autocratic leader sometimes has to be participative, and a reformer sometimes needs to act like an autocrat. But by thinking clearly about the different roles I've needed to assume at different times, I've been better able to tailor the way I make decisions, communicate with people, and manage my time so that I can address the most pressing needs of the organization at the moment.

The Autocrat

Autocracy, which I became acquainted with in the early stages of my career—even before I arrived at Blue Cross—is the most painful, least enjoyable style of management. Yet it has its place, especially in a turnaround situation. When a business needs to change relatively quickly, it's much more important to just make a decision and get people moving than it is to take the time to conduct a thorough analysis and attempt to influence others to come around to your way of thinking. Therefore, I would define the autocratic leader not as someone who bullies others needlessly but as the managerial equivalent of an emergency room surgeon, forced to do whatever it takes to save a patient's life. Autocracy often causes pain and arouses antagonism, and there is simply no way for the chief executive to escape the resentment and blame that will be directed toward him or her. The best the CEO can do to mitigate matters is to assume personal responsibility, act quickly, and stay focused on the mission at hand.

My first lessons in autocracy came during the 1970s, when I served as the director of the Illinois Department of Mental Health (from 1972 to 1975) and as the director of the Illinois Bureau of the Budget (from 1975 to 1976).

In the latter position, it was my job to cut the budget in accordance with top-down decisions made by the governor. At that time, many states and municipalities had lost their credit ratings, could not borrow money, and had to make devastating cuts in spending and services as a result. In Illinois, we relied on efficient planning to help us reduce our expenditures and retain our bond rating. By following directives from the top, we did not have to make drastic cuts in services.

In 1977, I went to work for the Carter administration as the chief administrator of the newly created U.S. Health Care Financing Administration. HCFA was charged with bringing under one roof the financing systems for Medicare (which was then part of the Social Security Administration) and Medicaid (which was then part of the Department of Health, Education, and Welfare). The two agencies, which provided health care coverage for the poor, duplicated each other somewhat, wasting taxpayers' money and generating conflicting health care regulations. My directive was to bring a measure of efficiency to the new organization by creating a coordinated approach to purchasing health care services for both Medicaid and Medicare.

Accordingly, I felt that one of the first, most important steps was to get all 4,600 people from both agencies to work at one location. A physical move would offer a chance to build efficiency into HCFA from the start: When workers change offices, their old patterns are disrupted. They meet new people, encounter varied perspectives, and, theoretically at least, suggest to one another different and better ways of doing things. Of course, the resistance to this plan was as predictable as it was loud. Some employees resented having to relocate from offices in Washington, DC, to a new workplace in

Baltimore. A few even complained to their representatives in Congress.

To protect the project from strangulation, I had to act autocratically. My mandate was clear, and I discovered a few useful tactics to get people to help me fulfill it. First, it became apparent to me that assuming the responsibility for this high-risk decision could have tremendous power. Once I said the magic words "If this doesn't work, it's on my head," the politicians and administrators who were objecting to the move began to cooperate and stopped threatening to obstruct the reorganization. Second, I used the element of surprise: Had we announced the consolidation of Medicare and Medicaid in advance, opponents would have had time to block or stall the move. So the staffs were merged during a congressional recess. The surprise worked—HCFA went on to become the Centers for Medicare & Medicaid Services, a unified government health care services agency located outside of Baltimore that today provides coverage and benefits for about 70 million people nationwide.

If my experience in state and federal government was autocracy boot camp, Blue Cross of California was the battleground. It was an extremely dysfunctional bureaucracy. The company was born of a merger in June 1982 between two separate Blue Cross organizations (one in northern California and one in southern California), each with its own administrative systems. Neither had annual budgeting or planning processes. By the mid-1980s, millions of customers had fled to alternate health plans because of escalating premiums and diminishing quality of service, and the organization was losing close to $1 million a day. Worse yet was the failure of many self-satisfied Blue Cross executives to identify with their customers. During my first week at the company, I asked senior managers what business the company was in. "We're in the business of being Blue Cross," they smugly responded.

With the company hemorrhaging money and with pressure from the board to turn things around quickly, I had to be the bad guy: Within 18 months, I was forced to lay off nearly half the company's 6,000 employees. I had no problem with getting rid of every one of the senior managers who had run the company into the ground. But it was painful to let go of the rank-and-file workers who were not responsible for the mismanagement. Equally painful was the realization that Blue Cross was at the brink of financial death; if things didn't change quickly, there would be no health care insurance for millions of Californians.

Certainly, the company acted humanely by providing laid-off workers with outplacement services and continued medical coverage, but on a personal level, it was unpleasant to see so many good people lose their jobs because of previous management's mistakes. It was clear, though, that if we responded too slowly or lost sight of the goal—to pull Blue Cross from intensive-care status—the remaining employees would ultimately lose their jobs, too.

Fortunately, this didn't happen. By 1989, the company was rebounding from its sizable losses in previous years—its finances were stabilizing, subscriber numbers were slowly coming back up, and earnings were increasing, too. By 1991, the company was reporting profits of more than $13 million per month, and in January 1993, we went public with WellPoint Health Networks, initially establishing the business as an operating subsidiary of Blue Cross of California and then recapitalizing the company in 1996 as the parent.

With the company stabilized and growing, my days of autocratic management were coming to a welcome end. As we began to focus more on creating innovative insurance products and on providing excellent customer service, "any decision" was no longer better than "no decision."

The Participative Leader

Now my primary role as CEO was to ensure the organization's long-term success. The company's priorities had changed, so the way I functioned had to change. I needed to help the company achieve an industry-leading position by participating in, but not actually making, day-to-day decisions. Autocratic orders wouldn't cut it anymore; the company was too big. The onus was on those Blue Cross–WellPoint associates who were closest to our customers and partners to make the right decisions and implement them based on their personal knowledge of the industry.

Participative leadership, a term coined by the late University of Michigan researcher Rensis Likert, requires that the CEO receive sufficient information from employees to make important strategic decisions but that he or she leave the implementation of strategy up to the line managers. In my experience, this form of leadership is best carried out by employing a methodology first articulated by consultants at McKinsey: Under loose-tight management, the development of goals, budgets, and strategies is strictly controlled from the top while staff is given free rein to meet those goals, as long as they stay on budget.

Here's how it works at WellPoint. Each year, WellPoint's executive management team sets four or five very clear goals for the company. An example might be "Leverage technology as a competitive advantage," or "Use innovation and service to increase our value to our customers." We lay out specific strategies for attaining each of the goals, and we print the objectives and the strategies, along with our overarching mission statement, on a pocket-size card to reinforce the message for all of our associates. Then each manager must take some responsibility for meeting the goals. For instance, if the goal were "Use innovation and service to increase our value to our customers," each division president would be required to develop innovative new products or ways to provide high-quality service to WellPoint's members, payers, brokers and agents, and health care providers— in such a way that the company would see a tangible bottom-line benefit.

If this high-level goal setting sounds like the same thing every company does ad nauseum, it may well be. The difference is that even though we require strict implementation of our strategies (tightness), we put few restrictions on how managers carry them out (looseness). By rigorously adhering to the budget and the established strategies, and by combing through the fine details, WellPoint line managers unearth surprising business opportunities that senior leaders cannot see.

Here is an example. Part of our corporate mission is to offer a choice of health care products that put individuals in control of their health and their financial future. So one of our goals is: "We will offer a choice of health services." In response, Mark Weinberg and Deborah Lachman, both senior leaders in charge of our services for small businesses, scratched their heads and said, "That's very nice, Leonard, but what do you mean by choice?" I didn't give them an explanation; it was up to them to use their knowledge of the market to figure it out. Their mandate was to provide more choice to customers while simultaneously realizing a 15% growth rate in the small-business segment. As long as what Mark and Debbie did stayed within regulatory and ethical bounds, the means were their own. They could hire whomever they wanted and could assign tasks however they wished, without an okay from me. If I disagreed with their choices, I would merely shake my head and keep my mouth shut.

The "tight" part of the equation came into play as Mark, Debbie, and their team charted their progress toward the goal. First, they developed a primary plan of attack (Plan A) and two contingency plans, then they set a series of milestones for each. Quarterly, monthly, weekly, and even daily, the group monitored its success in developing a new product that would give customers more choice. The information about everything the group was doing was logged into our company intranet so Mark, Debbie, their managers, and I could quickly check the progress against the milestones at any time. If they met or exceeded their plan, as most associates do, everything was fine. If they didn't, they would implement one of their two contingency plans (Plan B then Plan C). No one would tell them how to get their results in line with providing more choice to customers, but as senior officers, Mark and Debbie knew they could be out of a job if they didn't meet their goals.

Many who observe this loose-tight process wonder how people are able to do their work, given the amount of scenario planning and time required to develop, implement, and track goals. But employees tell me that the strict guidelines actually make it easier for them to manage their daily work because they never lose sight of their mandates. They understand their priorities.

Moreover, the research process that falls out of adhering to the budget and the goals sometimes yields innovative ideas. Mark and Debbie, for example, conducted a careful review of the available information on small-business insurance plans and discovered that no one was offering individual employees a choice of coverage. Instead, small businesses were buying one-size-fits-all plans that could satisfy general needs but that didn't cover special ones. Their further research revealed much about individual concerns within small businesses: Owners, for example, tend to prefer top-of-the-line service that covers, say, their acupuncture treatments. Younger workers just want to know that if they break a leg snowboarding, their hospital care will be paid for. And diabetic employees want their chronic-care services affordably covered by an HMO, especially if their condition worsens.

After collecting this data, Mark and Debbie wondered if it might be possible to average health care insurance costs across a small business. If the owner was willing to pay a little more for expensive premium coverage and the young person opted for catastrophic insurance only, the small company would be able to afford a plan that could cover chronic illnesses (like diabetes), too—all for the

Being a participative leader isn't always easy, because it requires letting go. I have to trust all the people who work for me to make wise management decisions.

same price as their current insurance. Working with Blue Cross's actuaries, Mark and Debbie and their associates analyzed in detail the sales, trends, and historical growth of our product lines and services. Several what-if models led them to discover that, in fact, it would be possible to offer a mixed bag of coverage to all the customers in their market segment for a competitive price. The team developed EmployeeElect, an umbrella service that lets employees at small businesses choose from nine types of health care coverage to meet their individual needs. They presented me with the idea, and I wholeheartedly approved. Today, EmployeeElect is one of our most popular plans.

Our tight processes take time, but they work. In fact, they're helping us win the health care industry's tortoise-and-hare race. In the early-to-mid-1990s, our competitors were boasting aggressive growth rates of 30% to 50% and pursuing lots of M&A deals. But our budgetary processes told us that it wasn't tenable to sustain that kind of rapid growth and that we should maintain our growth rate at 15% annually with a more conservative effort, steering clear of blockbuster acquisitions and faddish expansions. The end result? We have met or exceeded investors' expectations for 32 consecutive quarters while some of our competitors have had to restructure their businesses or have become acquisition targets themselves.

Being a participative leader isn't always easy, particularly for a recovering autocrat like myself. It requires letting go. I have to trust all the people who work for me to make wise management decisions. They have *A reformer demonstrates* to be insightful enough to *what is possible. He or she* correct mistakes on their *defies convention and* own, without input from *stubbornly tries to make* me. And participative *the world a better place.* leadership is particularly tricky in a company that's geographically dispersed, like ours is. You have to believe that regional managers know what's best for the customers and employees in their local areas.

The Reformer

Now that WellPoint's ability to deliver on its promises to customers and investors has become more predictable, I have been able to spend more time practicing a reformer style of leadership. A reformer demonstrates what is possible. He or she defies convention and stubbornly tries to make the world a better place.

I feel as though my personal challenge is to change the universally disliked managed-care industry so consumers will feel they can trust their insurance providers. Doing this requires taking some chances. In July 1998, WellPoint undertook a drive to make the allergy drug Claritin and several other antihistamines available over the counter. The idea sprang from our tight planning process: The biggest threat to our ability to keep our prescription drug benefits affordable is the spiraling costs of the medications themselves. Of course, we do everything we can to shift these costs to those prescription drugs that offer the most value to our customers. That means offering generic drugs where appropriate and educating our members about the importance of keeping to their prescription drug regimens. But we needed to do more.

Robert Seidman, WellPoint's chief pharmacy officer, looked carefully at our prescription costs and found that one of the most commonly prescribed categories of drugs among our subscribers was allergy medicines such as Claritin, Allegra, and Zyrtec. These medicines are sold over the counter in most countries and, when taken at the recommended dosage, can have fewer side effects than nonprescription allergy remedies. Rob noted that a single, first-time prescription for Claritin, for example, including the visit to the doctor, cost $165. Refills were $65 each. The most popular over-the-counter alternative to Claritin is Benadryl, which is available for about $4.50. Benadryl is just as effective as Claritin in treating allergy symptoms, but its sedating side effects make it unsafe to take while driving or operating machinery. In fact, hundreds of people die each year in Benadryl-related accidents. All of which led us to wonder: "Why should patients and insurers have to pay $165 for a prescription drug that has minimal side effects while it costs $4.50 to get a drug whose side effects can harm you?"

Rob began scrutinizing the FDA rules for converting a drug from being available only by prescription to being available over the counter. In the process, he discovered two things: First, no company outside the pharmaceutical industry had ever petitioned the FDA to do such a thing. Second, there was no rule or law preventing a non-pharmaceutical company from doing so. Rob also discovered a little-known law that said any drug that can be taken for a condition that can be self-diagnosed, that will successfully treat the condition, and that is safe and effective for the consumer when used without a doctor's supervision, does not require a prescription. Accordingly, we submitted a petition to remove Claritin, Allegra, and Zyrtec from the prescription list, and an FDA panel approved it. Once an FDA commissioner approves the panel's recommendation, the drugs will be available over the counter, and the overall cost of prescriptions will drop for patients and insurers. More important, consumers will be able to afford an effective allergy medicine that will not harm them.

Our objective was not to hurt the drug companies; we're in favor of any prescription drugs that truly help patients and add value to the health care system. But the petition seemed like a sensible move, one that would remove unnecessary costs from the system. In the process, I also discovered that it is possible for a corporate leader to create real, industrial-scale change.

Being a reformer is gratifying, but it has its challenges, too. The demands on my time are much greater than they were when my job was focused exclusively on WellPoint's well-being. I spend 30% of my time meeting with people outside the company, primarily industry and government representatives, discussing health care practices and policies. And as a reformer, I've become the point person for their tough questions. Some people seem to think I carry a crystal ball that allows me to peer into the future of health care in the United States. I don't, despite the fact that I spend most of my time—on planes, in the office, and sometimes in bed at two in the morning—thinking about it.

IN EACH PHASE OF MY leadership journey, I've had a concrete goal—consolidate two large organizations, fight for corporate survival, drive my company to achieve success in the marketplace, or change the health care industry for the better. Being able to shift my management style as each of these new challenges appeared has been extremely effective for me. It isn't always easy to put on a different leadership cap or alter the way you assess a business situation. Under pressure, most people fall back on the style or approach that worked in the last crisis they faced. But old approaches rarely work in new and demanding situations.

Ultimately, the demands of the marketplace have shaped my leadership journey. Indeed, I've learned that by paying attention to processes and aligning teams so that they are as dedicated to fulfilling goals as I am, it's possible to create something that lasts much longer than anything carved in ice.

Originally published in October 2002
Reprint R0210B

What Titans Can Teach Us

RICHARD S. TEDLOW

Executive Summary

THE LEGENDARY TITANS of American business could
be scheming and ruthless. We surely wouldn't want to
emulate them in every particular. But a business leader
doesn't have to strive for titanhood to benefit from the
lessons such giants have to teach. And perhaps by studying them, we can learn to spot titans in the making, a
valuable skill for leaders scanning the landscape for
potential partners or dangerous competitors.

Focusing on the experiences of seven great innovators—steel magnate Andrew Carnegie, Kodak's George
Eastman, automaker Henry Ford, Intel's Robert Noyce,
Revlon's Charles Revson, Wal-Mart's Sam Walton, and
IBM's Thomas J. Watson—the author argues that many of
their traits are replicable by mere mortals. A handful of
simple principles were woven into their lives: Have the
courage to bet on your vision of market potential. Shape

115

your vision of the market into a mission for the company and consistent messages for customers, employees, and investors. Deliver more than you promise. Be dedicated to your company, even to a fault. And don't look back.

Enlivening his narrative with such details as Walton's hula dance on Wall Street and Eastman's succinct suicide note—"My work is done—why wait?"—the author shows that the titans thought about their companies every waking moment and expected the same of their employees. They were willing to pay whatever price was needed to create something new in the business world.

Whether they led through inspiration or intimidation, a clear mission and consistent messages were keys to making their dreams reality. So were a limitless sense of what they had to offer and an unflinching commitment to the fulfillment of their destinies. Their certainty in the face of uncertainty, skepticism, and even ridicule was a beacon for attracting and motivating followers.

F IRST THINGS FIRST: I'm not going to make the case in this article that the legendary titans of American business offer a template of leadership lessons for all of us to follow. Many were individuals we wouldn't want to emulate, at least in every particular. They could be scheming and, more than occasionally, ruthless. Indeed, in many instances they were as titanic in the problems they created—especially the interpersonal problems—as in the empires they built.

Furthermore, most of us couldn't emulate these legends even if we tried. They were wildly opportunistic, ambitious beyond measure, and often just plain brilliant. While these attributes are useful and even admirable for businesspeople, the genuine giants of enterprise had them to a unique degree—which partly explains why they were titans and most other people are not.

That said, a business leader doesn't have to strive for titanhood to benefit from the lessons a titan has to teach. We can pick and choose the characteristics that will help make our companies more successful. Perhaps just as important, we can learn to spot titans in the making, a valuable skill for leaders scanning the landscape for potential business partners or successors—or on the lookout for dangerous competitors.

What do I mean by "titan?" For me, the term encompasses those executives—there have been perhaps 30 or 40 in the history of American business—who created or transformed industries and in the process changed the world. All of them grew rich as they did so. Most of them became household names. Is someone like Jack Welch a member of this elite club? The answer: We just don't know yet. You can only identify a titan with historical perspective—which is what makes the subject so fascinating for me, a business historian.

For the past three decades, I have studied the giants of American enterprise. Using my database of detailed biographical and company information on 250 outstanding business executives, I have identified the individuals whom I call titans and then looked for common denominators among the select few.

A defining characteristic of the titans was their ability to tell the difference between the seemingly impossible and the genuinely impossible.

This article draws on the experiences of seven of the titans: steel magnate Andrew Carnegie; George Eastman, the father of mass-market photography;

automaker Henry Ford; IBM's Thomas J. Watson; Charles Revson, founder of cosmetics maker Revlon; Wal-Mart's Sam Walton; and Robert Noyce, the cofounder of Intel.

These seven were very different people. Eastman and Noyce led primarily through inspiration; Carnegie and Watson led mainly by intimidation. Walton, the optimist, could light up a room; Revson, the pessimist, could light up a room by leaving it. Noyce helped ensure a successful future for Intel by working in close partnership with two successors, Gordon Moore and Andy Grove, whose talents complemented his and suited the company in its next stages of growth. Ford, by contrast, became vindictive as he aged and nearly destroyed his company. (Different though they were, we must note that they were all not only male but also Caucasian. There are women and minorities in business today whom future generations will regard as titans, but their impact on the business scene is too recent to permit the historical perspective we need to make that judgment.)

Though titans are a varied lot, we can still tease some common traits out of their disparate personalities and lives. Some of these reflect their particular genius. For example, a defining characteristic of these men was their ability to tell the difference between the seemingly impossible and the genuinely impossible. Other traits are similarly relevant to their business success but are more replicable by mere mortals. In studying their careers, we can see a handful of principles that were woven into their lives:

- Have the courage to bet on your vision of market potential.

- Shape your vision of the market into a mission for the company and consistent messages for customers, employees, and investors.

- Deliver more than you promise.

- Be dedicated, even to a fault, to your company.

- Don't look back.

The following stories—yes, stories; I'm a historian, not a management consultant—illustrate ways in which the titans lived these five principles. I would not advise anyone to try to mimic a particular titan. But they did drive their companies to success with stunning power. What they did worked, and there is plenty they can teach us.

A Camera for Everyone

George Eastman seems an unlikely creator of mass-market photography, an innovation that enabled ordinary people to create visual records of their lives without the expense of hiring professional photographers or portrait painters. His first job was as an office boy in an insurance firm—the death of his debt-ridden father and the straitened financial circumstances of his family had forced him to go to work in 1868 at the age of 13. He was paid $3 a week, and his responsibilities included cleaning out the cuspidors.

Not long thereafter, Eastman took a job as a clerk at the Rochester (New York) Savings Bank, where he quickly moved up to second assistant bookkeeper. In 1877, after spending almost a decade in the working world, he bought a camera. Four years later, he left the bank to devote himself fully to starting a photography business. Eventually, his business would transform the complicated contraptions used by professional photographers into light little boxes anyone could afford.

Even after he threw himself exclusively into photography, it took time for Eastman to comprehend that there was a mass market for picture taking. When he started in the business, cameras were expensive, costing roughly $50. They required considerable expertise to operate. Few people in the early 1880s even thought about taking photographs. But what if photography could be made both cheap and easy? No one knew. No one even knew this was a question worth asking.

In the late 1880s, though, Eastman began to believe that he "could reach the general public and create a new class of patrons"—that is, democratize photography while creating a lucrative new market. "Success," he wrote in 1890, "means millions." In 1894, he said that "the manifest destiny of the Eastman Kodak Company is to be the largest manufacturer of photographic materials in the world or else go to pot." In 1900, Eastman brought out the Kodak Brownie, which sold for $1. One of the great product introductions in American business history, the Brownie allowed Eastman to realize his vision: photography for everyone.

How did Eastman know there was a mass market for photography when few people had ever seen a camera? Similarly, how did Carnegie know that steel, once sold by the pound, would in the new industrialized world be sold by the ton? How did Ford know to stick with low-priced cars in the early years of the industry when rival automakers in America and Europe kept moving upmarket? How did Watson know that the future lay in the small branch of his company that made tabulating machines? How did Revson know in 1932, during the depths of the Depression, that there was a profitable market for high-fashion nail polish? How did Walton know that small towns could support big stores? How did Noyce know that the integrated circuit, of which he was the coinventor, would change the world?

They just knew. They sensed they were on to something. It's as simple, and as complex, as that—not very encouraging for those trying to emulate their success. An intuitive sense of market potential is not the sort of thing you can study hard to learn.

But if the titans possessed that jagged streak of lightning called genius, they also had something else: Each had the courage to bet on his vision. Achieving a breakthrough insight is one thing. Acting on it is quite another. These monumental figures were more than men of potential, they were kinetic. They refused to be scared off by precedent.

Eastman's actions reflected his belief that his company's "manifest destiny" was to succeed on a grand scale. Walton, who built giant Wal-Mart stores across the land and around the world, wasn't deterred by the fact that no one saw a huge retailing opportunity in rural areas and small towns. Ford didn't care that the United States had few passable roads for his new automobile. As Noyce once said, "Don't be encumbered by history. Go out and do something wonderful."

Hula on Wall Street

The date was March 15, 1984. The place was Wall Street, the financial capital of the world. The man was Samuel Moore Walton, at the time the nation's second-richest citizen. The event was a hula performance.

Walton had made a bet with his chief operating officer, David Glass, that Wal-Mart could not achieve a pretax profit of 8% on sales. In 1983, the company met that target, and Glass insisted that Walton keep his promise to do the hula on Wall Street. And this bet was not going to be paid off on the sly in the dark of night. Glass saw to it that there was a grass skirt for Walton to put on over his suit, musicians and young professional hula dancers to accompany him, and, of course, full media attention.

By this time, Walton and Wal-Mart were well known and respected in the investment community and throughout a large part of the nation. But here was the company's CEO flying in from Arkansas and engaging in what Walton himself later characterized as a "pretty primitive publicity stunt." Although such stunts—at stores, at headquarters, for customers, for suppliers, for employees, for the media—were a staple at Wal-Mart, Walton had to confess that this particular display genuinely embarrassed him.

Why, then, did he do it? True, he had made a bet and had lost. But no one could have forced Sam Walton to pay up. He could have said that it wasn't appropriate for the CEO of one of the nation's fastest-growing companies to make a fool of himself in the middle of the financial district. He could have cited his age, 65, and his recent bout with leukemia—not to mention the 28-degree temperature on the day of the dance. Or he could have simply let Glass know that if he liked working for the leading retailer in Bentonville, Arkansas, he'd better let the bet die a quiet death. But despite his wealth and power, Walton kept his promise—and he did it to make a point.

Or rather several points. Sam (one naturally falls into referring to this multibillionaire by his first name) originally saw a market opportunity in offering customers outside big cities quality goods at low prices. This vision became the company's mission, which was articulated in a memorable message: "Always the low price—*always*." Clearly, a key to maintaining low prices is keeping costs down. So instead of taking out an ad in the *Wall Street*

Journal, Walton publicized Wal-Mart's achievement with a publicity device that cost almost nothing. A penny saved on advertising was a penny that could be passed along to the customer. In fact, the main cost associated with the event was to Walton's dignity—which he would never have placed above the good of the company.

But Walton had more than customers in mind when he did his hula. For decades, he had been preaching to employees that rank does not have its privileges. In his mind, the thousands of salespeople on the floor were as important as top executives, because Wal-Mart's primary contact with its customers was through these low-wage employees. His dance signaled that he was a down-to-earth guy who didn't have an inflated view of himself.

By showing up in a hula skirt on Wall Street, Sam Walton showed he was willing to put the company's interests above his own—just as he wanted his employees to do.

Walton also praised outlandish behavior among employees because it stimulated creativity and helped make Wal-Mart "a fun proposition." He endlessly insisted that you could learn from anybody, and having fun was one way that the thousands of anybodies at Wal-Mart did their teaching. Walton had a special genius for transforming anybodies into somebodies. When the silly season rolled around, Walton didn't merely cheer from the sidelines, he was a player-coach.

Finally, Walton showed employees that he was willing to put the company's interests above his own—just as he wanted them to do. He knew that the speed of the boss is the speed of the gang, and his sense of fairness would not permit him to demand that others sacrifice for the company if he were unwilling to do so.

The hula wasn't staged on Wall Street by chance. There was also a message for investors and analysts: I may not look like the most sophisticated executive in the world, but I'm a winner. Actions speak louder than words, and losers don't pull stunts like this. Margaret Gilliam, at the time an analyst for First Boston and one of the first to realize that Wal-Mart was a company with a future, did not have to travel far to photograph Sam in his grass skirt.

By walking his talk, Walton, in a single act, sent multiple messages to multiple constituencies. Although other titans may have used more conventional means, they all had a similar missionary zeal, which they communicated through clear and consistent messages.

George Eastman's ambition to bring photography to the people was reflected in the advertising slogan for the Brownie: "You push the button. We do the rest." Pithy to the point of poetry, it communicated to customers that photography was no longer a mysterious black art presided over by secretive professionals telling you to keep perfectly still while they mixed miraculous concoctions of chemicals to make your image appear on a glass plate.

Tom Watson's mission for IBM employees was reduced to a single word: Think. Or, more accurately, THINK. The word reflected the intellectual foundation of the technology-driven company.

Tom Watson's mission for IBM employees was reduced to a single word: think. Or, more accurately, THINK. The word reflected the technology-driven company's intellectual foundation. (It also said something about Watson's leadership style. When he plastered THINK signs all over the company, he wasn't saying, "Think for yourself." There was no mistaking he meant, "Think like me.")

A Giant Pay Raise

On January 5, 1914, Henry Ford stood by quietly in his office as an associate read a news release to reporters from three Detroit newspapers:

"The Ford Motor Co., the greatest and most successful automobile manufacturing company in the world, will, on Jan. 12, inaugurate the greatest revolution in the matter of rewards for its workers ever known to the industrial world. At one stroke it will reduce the hours of labor from nine to eight, and add to every man's pay a share of the profits of the house. The smallest amount to be received by a man 22 years old and upwards will be $5 per day."

The language of the press release was self-congratulatory, but deservedly so. Three months earlier, Ford workers had received a 13% wage increase to $2.34 a day. Now, without violence, without pressure from a union, the company was more than doubling an already competitive wage.

Ford saw the press release as merely a good local story, so he distributed it only to the local press. But it became the biggest news story to originate in Detroit up to that time, and it made Henry Ford famous around the world.

There were, it should be said, business reasons for the big jump in workers' salaries. Because of growing mechanization, work in the plant was becoming increasingly stultifying; the turnover rate at Ford was a staggering 370% in 1913. A more stable and better-paid workforce could—and ultimately did—result in production efficiencies. But these were not the only reasons for the pay hike. Henry Ford simply felt it was the thing to do. As one newspaper described him at the time, he "has declined to forget that the distance between overalls and broadcloth is very short." With the pay raise, he was delivering far more than he had promised—indeed, more than any of his employees might have reasonably expected.

The titans delivered more than they promised to investors, as well. The sister of one of Ford's first partners put $100 into his company. Less than two decades later, Rosetta Couzens Hauss, a schoolteacher in Chatham, Ontario, received $262,036.67 for that $100. And true titans could generate big rewards for investors even when their companies encountered bumps along the road. One Intel manager recalls the faith that the investment community placed in Noyce: "Bob could stand up in front of a roomful of securities analysts and tell them we were facing a number of major problems in our business—and the stock would go up five points."

More subtly, the breakthrough products or services that the titans created also delivered more than customers ever expected. During the Depression, Revson introduced the Revlon brand of coordinated nail polish and lipstick, which gave women "matching lips and fingertips." Helena Rubinstein derided the brightly colored nail polish as trashy. But by turning nail enamel from a commodity into a fashion item, he gave women of modest means an unexpected way to feel special. As Revson said, "in the factory, we make cosmetics; in the store, we sell hope."

Split Personality

Andrew Carnegie is one of the most seductive of the business titans. He embodied the American dream, rising from rags not to riches—but to richest. In 1848, Carnegie was forced to emigrate from Scotland, where his father, a hand-loom weaver, had been put out of work by the technology of steam power. Carnegie would go on to master, rather than be mastered by, technology.

At 13, he got a job at $1.20 a week in a steam-driven textile mill in Pittsburgh. He left to work in a telegraph office and taught himself Morse code. His next move was to the Pennsylvania Railroad, the spine of American enterprise in the mid-nineteenth century. With the help of Tom Scott, a mentor who became a surrogate father, Carnegie quickly rose to become superintendent of the railroad's western division. By the time of the Civil War, Carnegie had mastered the two forces that were changing the world: the telegraph and the railroad.

After making a small fortune as an investor during the 1860s, Carnegie was hit with a searing insight. Technological breakthroughs, most notably the Bessemer process, opened up the possibility of producing steel in undreamed-of quantities. Knowing railroads and their desperate need for strong, all-weather rails, Carnegie was convinced that steel would change the material basis of civilization in the last quarter of the nineteenth century. His conviction proved justified.

Carnegie was charming and witty with a puckish sense of humor. Unlike contemporary "robber barons" such as J.P. Morgan or John D. Rockefeller, he wanted to be liked and knew how to make himself likable. However, he had neither compunction nor hesitation about breaking the eggs that went into his omelette.

Take his early mentor, Tom Scott, the man who lifted Carnegie out of the obscurity of a telegraph office and into the upper reaches of the Pennsylvania Railroad, who taught the unschooled immigrant how to invest and financed his first investment. In 1873, when Scott came to him for financial help to stave off bankruptcy, the wealthy Carnegie summarily turned him down. He could be similarly strict with his partners—who were partners in name only. Carnegie owned the majority of his com-

pany and doled out dividends parsimoniously. His partners worked long days while he took extended vacations.

Perhaps most telling, Carnegie was ruthless with the
workers in his gigantic mills. He fancied himself a great
friend of labor. "My experience," he wrote in 1886, "has
been that trades-unions, upon the whole, are beneficial
both to labor and to capital." He also declared that there
"is an unwritten law among the best workmen: 'Thou
shalt not take thy neighbor's job.'" Not many employers
were saying that sort of thing in 1886, and Carnegie was
lionized among workers in many industries.

Six years later, Carnegie, conveniently on vacation in
Britain, allowed his partner Henry Clay Frick to break the
union at the company's Homestead Plant. Pinkerton
detectives were hired. Scab labor was brought in. Lives
were lost. The Amalgamated Association of Iron and Steel
Workers met with complete defeat. As one of Carnegie's
executives put it, "The Amalgamated placed a tax on
improvements, therefore the Amalgamated had to go."

Like most of America's business titans, Carnegie paid
a high personal price for his complete dedication to his
company's success and to his own ambition. The price for him was the sharp split between what he wanted to be—or at least saw himself as—and what tremendous success in business demanded that he be. Carnegie sought the affection of his

The titans led their companies to greatness by thinking about them every waking moment. George Eastman committed suicide and left a note that read: "To my friends: My work is done—why wait?"

friends, partners, and workers. Yet, in the end, he alien-
ated many because his loyalty was to his company first,
last, and above all.

Carnegie was not alone among the titans in his single-minded dedication to his ambition. Most of them had wives, clubs, hobbies, and philanthropic endeavors. But they led their companies to greatness by thinking about them every waking moment and by expecting the same from their employees. They were willing to pay the price needed to create something new in the business world.

Tom Watson retired from IBM in May 1956—and died in June 1956, having refused potentially lifesaving surgery for an intestinal problem. George Eastman committed suicide and left a note that read: "To my friends: My work is done—why wait?" Eastman's note may have been a bit misleading. At 77, he hadn't worked regularly for years. He had traveled extensively to foreign countries in his retirement. His health was failing. But the sentiments certainly captured the fact that, as with Watson, his company had been the center of his life.

It is perhaps noteworthy that Eastman, unlike some other titans, didn't let an all-encompassing focus on the success of his business undermine his personal values and friendships. As Eastman's first financial backer and partner observed, "You are a queer cuss, Geo, and I know you never want any sympathy or comfort from your friends. But I want you to know that I, for one, appreciate the mountains of care and responsibility that you are constantly called to overcome. And if I never express it in words, it may be a source of comfort to you to know that I am always with you heart and hand."

Starting Over at 40

John Patterson, the founder of National Cash Register Company and Tom Watson's first boss, dealt with people in three stages. First, he shattered a man's spirit and obliterated his previous identity and self-conception. Then he built him up, buttressed his self-esteem, and paid him lavishly. Then he fired him.

That's a fair description of Watson's career path at NCR. He joined the company as a salesman in Buffalo, New York, in 1895 when he was 21. He devoted himself to NCR and its mercurial leader, doing whatever it took to get ahead, for almost two decades. In 1913, he found his head on the chopping block.

It wasn't, to put it mildly, an easy period in Watson's life. He was 40 years old and newly married with an infant son. He also had serious legal problems, having been convicted, along with other NCR executives, of criminal violations of the Sherman Act for his unquestioning adherence to some of Patterson's less attractive business practices. Although the conviction was later overturned on appeal, Watson at the time faced a year in jail and a $5,000 fine.

Watson took a job with an unknown company called Computing-Tabulating-Recording, a motley and directionless conglomerate that made scales (computing), adding and sorting machines (tabulating), and time clocks (recording). Soon he was running the company, rechristened International Business Machines. His focus on the relatively small tabulating division put IBM on the road to becoming the preeminent name in what came to be known as computers. Significantly, Watson didn't carry a grudge against Patterson, who taught him many of the sales techniques that later contributed to IBM's success. As Thomas J. Watson, Jr., Watson's son and successor as CEO at IBM, once remarked: "Oddly, Dad never complained [of Patterson's firing him] and revered Mr. Patterson until the day he died."

Titans don't look back. When they suffer a failure, they get over it. Most know the valleys as well as the peaks—but they never perceive a chasm, no matter how daunting, to be the Valley of Death. They don't ruminate. They are incapable of being discouraged.

And whatever problems they have faced in the past, they're not afraid of the future, because they plan to play a big role in creating it. While not necessarily arrogant, they do have staggering confidence in themselves. For example, when William Shockley, the famed coinventor of the transistor, asked the unknown Bob Noyce to interview for a job at his new semiconductor company, Noyce left his job at Philco in Philadelphia and bought a house in Palo Alto, California—*before* the interview. This self-confidence is contagious and serves the titan superbly well when things start going badly, as they did for every one of these men at one time or another.

For example, Intel's first two products, introduced in 1969, were technically advanced but commercially unsuccessful. Rumors began to circulate that if Intel didn't have a success soon, it would be in trouble. Undaunted, Noyce pressed on, and Intel brought out the first in a long string of blockbuster products. Eastman was passed over for first assistant bookkeeper at the Rochester Savings Bank because of nepotism. Eastman, who had an acute sense of fairness, was outraged. Walton lost his first store—a thriving five-and-dime in Newport, Arkansas—to the landlord's son because he failed to notice that his lease didn't include a renewal clause. Ford founded two companies that failed before he created the Ford Motor Company. Revson was living hand-to-mouth, thanks to a string of dead-end jobs, when he founded Revlon in 1932.

One clear lesson that everyone can take from the titans is that they didn't blame others—or the universe—for their problems. They may have been downcast or temporarily angry with themselves. But they didn't whine that life was unfair. They believed the world was essentially a just place that would reward their effort and, ultimately, yield to their genius. Any setback was a temporary misunderstanding by the cosmos.

There is no formula for business greatness. There are, however, themes that recur in the conduct of business titans. Whether they led through inspiration or intimidation, a clear mission and consistent messages were keys to making their dreams a reality. So were a limitless sense of what they had to offer and an unflinching commitment to the fulfillment of their destinies.

Their certainty in the face of an uncertain, sometimes derisive, world can be a beacon for attracting and motivating followers. Their message is not inclusive, however. The individuals I have studied didn't create organizations designed for everyone. If you wanted to work for one of them, you had to buy into the mission and spread the message. Otherwise, you belonged elsewhere.

As we have seen, there may be good reasons not to try to become a titan yourself. But whatever your aim, it's good to be able to recognize a titan. We can also take inspiration and ideas from these giants of enterprise and their common achievement: business success through the writing (and enforcing) of their own rules.

Originally published in December 2001
Reprint R0111E

Where Leadership Starts

ROBERT A. ECKERT

Executive Summary

IN MAY 2000, BOB ECKERT SAT on a plane bound
for the West Coast and thought to himself, "What have I
done?" He was about to become CEO of Mattel, a
struggling company in an industry he knew nothing
about. And he was facing unrealistic expectations not
only from Wall Street but also from Mattel's 30,000
employees, who hoped for an effective leader yet
feared sweeping change.

How did this former CEO of Kraft Foods address
employees' anxiety, gain their trust, and start to turn Mat-
tell around? By using the concept of "mealtime." When
people gather together to share a meal, they are nourished in both body and spirit. They become face-to-face
equals who exchange opinions, ask questions, receive
answers, and share ideas. Eckert knew that he had to
build brands and cut costs, but he found that the most

133

crucial and challenging task was to make others feel comfortable enough to share their metaphorical meals with him. And he found his favorite place to share these metaphorical—and actual—meals was the employee cafeteria.

To make each meal a success, Eckert practiced what he calls "setting the table," which means preparing the atmosphere for honest dialogue by drawing on a set of tools—utensils, if you will—designed to quell apprehension. These include naming the source of tension and calling for honesty; deferring, when appropriate, to the other person's realm of expertise; and recognizing common experience.

In this article, Eckert tells the story of his first steps from "food" guy to "toy" guy and describes what it takes to fit into the strange new world of another company.

IN MAY OF LAST YEAR, as I was sitting on an airplane flying to the West Coast, I thought to myself, "What have I done?" I had just quit my job at Kraft Foods—the only company I had ever worked for—where I had enjoyed a long and successful career and had made lifelong friends. Now I was moving not only myself but also my family from Chicago to Los Angeles, where I was about to become CEO of a troubled company in an industry I didn't know anything about.

The company I was joining is the world's largest toy maker, and its power brands—Barbie, Hot Wheels, American Girl, and Fisher-Price—are household names. Despite these strengths, however, Mattel had lost its focus. It was losing up to a million dollars a day on the Learning Company, a software firm acquired during my

predecessor's reign. Mattel was borrowing money to stay
afloat, and several top managers—including the CIO,
head of operations, and head of communications—had
left. The company had been without a CEO for five
months. Morale was at an all-time low, and the stock
price wasn't far behind. Mattel no longer knew what it
was or what it stood for. It was time to refocus.

The company's turnaround is now in full swing, and
while there will undoubtedly be bumps along the road,
we have made solid progress. The Learning Company has
been sold. Costs are down, and revenue is up. Market
share has increased both in the United States and abroad
for the first time in three years. And investors have
rewarded us. According to the feedback I've received,
stockholders, the investment community, our board, and
our customers are encouraged by Mattel's progress.
Indeed, Wall Street is starting to consider how we'll
spend the cash we're generating—not how long we'll stay
afloat. Best of all, Mattel's 30,000 employees—the company's most important asset—have a renewed sense of
dedication to Mattel's mission: to create and market the
world's premier toy brands for today and tomorrow.

Like any new CEO who walks into a struggling company, I was facing unrealistic expectations from all kinds
of people who'd never met me, not just Wall Street analysts and customers but also Mattel's employees around
the world. On the one hand, employees hoped for someone who could single-handedly turn the company
around; on the other hand, they feared someone who
would initiate sweeping and unilateral change. As an
industry outsider, I found myself in a particularly tough
position. I had anticipated some likely questions: "What
does this 'food' guy know about toys? What does he
know about Mattel?" (See "Jumping Industries: Ten

Tips" at the end of this article.) Of course, I had done my homework. I had read everything there was to read about Mattel, including hundreds of analyst reports, articles, and press materials. I had scoured Web sites and visited chat rooms. And I had formulated a clear and concise plan of action that included three components I believed would get Mattel back on track: Build brands. Cut costs. Develop people.

You might assume that the first two steps were most critical to Mattel's survival. But for me, focusing on people proved to be the most crucial—and challenging—task. In this case, the emotional intelligence I'd developed over the years was even more important to my success than my traditional, analytic managerial skills were. As the new guy, I realized that every first encounter with a Mattel employee had the potential to be fraught with tension, and I felt it was my responsibility to do everything possible to reduce it. Surprisingly, I found that in each situation, recognizing my own lack of knowledge about the company's people and culture—in effect, allowing employees to be the "boss" in certain situations—actually helped me lead.

To gain my colleagues' trust, I had to practice what I call "setting the table." By this I mean preparing the atmosphere for honest, collegial dialogue by drawing on a set of tools—utensils, if you will—designed to quell any sense of apprehension. These tools include naming the source of tension and calling for honesty; deferring, when appropriate, to the other person's realm of expertise; and recognizing common experience.

I used most of these approaches consciously, but others were unconscious; it became clear to me that I had used certain tools only in retrospect or when people pointed them out to me. I've found all of them to be effective in demonstrating to people that despite the change in leadership direction my arrival represented, the company was about to change for the better.

Knives, Forks, and Spoons

Hailing as I do from the food industry, the concept of "mealtime" provides a good set of metaphors for the style of management I like to practice. When people gather together to share a meal, they are nourished not only in body but also in spirit. They become face-to-face equals who exchange opinions, ask questions, receive answers, and share ideas. As I thought about various interactions during my first days at Mattel, I realized that many meetings that set the stage for our company's change of direction occurred during meals. My goal coming into Mattel was to make others comfortable enough to share their metaphorical meals with me. For these meals to be a success, however, the table had to be set properly.

After completing my talks with the search committee and finishing my extensive research on Mattel's product lines and business practices, there was one thing missing: I hadn't laid my eyes on any Mattel employees. I could not even think of accepting the position until I got a sense of the people and the culture. So before I was hired, I found myself sitting across the table from Alan Kaye, senior vice president of human resources. The recruiter and the board had agreed that I should meet Alan privately, so we met in Tucson, Arizona, for breakfast. As you can imagine, we were both apprehensive. I was wary of giving up a good job to head a company facing enormous problems. And I sensed that Alan was equally anxious about meeting his prospective boss.

In this case, "setting the table" required me to use the important tool of verbalizing the source of tension and asking for honesty in an effort to reduce it. As we began our meal, the atmosphere was friendly, but vaguely awkward. At one point in the conversation, Alan confessed to me that the company had never had training or employee-development programs—something in which I fervently believe. I was surprised by his admission and sensed that, in the back of his mind, Alan was wondering whether I'd blame him for the lack of such programs.

"Alan," I said over my raisin bran, "I know this is strange for both of us. I want this to be a good conversation—to get everything on the table as truthfully as we can. As far as I'm concerned, you are my HR guy. That means we have to have a very honest, two-way conversation about what's most important—that is, about Mattel." Having vocalized the discomfort inherent in the situation, I saw Alan relax. He now felt comfortable enough to open up.

In retrospect, I realize that in setting this particular table, I also used another tool: focusing the discussion not on my opinions or myself but on the other person's area of expertise. I picked an area in which Alan, not I, was the expert—and that was Mattel's human-resources function. Certainly, I could have asked about the company's balance sheet and cash flow, but finances were not Alan's strong suit—nor was that the kind of information I needed. Had the conversation focused on numbers, I would never have heard answers to critical questions like, How would Alan describe the current culture? Who were the important players? What was their state of mind? What did Alan think needed to happen?

After I accepted the position, I hopped on a plane and set off to meet the other 29,999 employees. When I arrived in Los Angeles, I had a chance to dine with Mattel's senior-management team, and I found myself setting the table again. At that dinner, I could only assume that most of the team members were actively wondering about their future with Mattel. Though the meeting was friendly and open, it was also highly charged. After all, I was an interloper about to assume the reins from a team of brilliant, talented people who, in the absence of a CEO, had run the company superbly.

I listened carefully to the words and tone of these managers as they spoke to me and to one another. As usual, I invited everyone to ask me very direct questions, and they took me up on the offer. There was one particularly telling moment when a senior manager laid everything on the table by saying, "So, Bob, what are you going to bring to the company?" I thought for a moment and looked at her carefully. "Look," I said, "if Mattel turns around, it will be because of your efforts as much as mine. But as the CEO, I will be the one to get all the credit, because that's how Wall Street works. I want you to know that I will try to deflect that credit and recognize the contributions you and your teams have made." In this case, I used the tool of deferring to my colleague, which disarmed the situation.

I needed an icebreaker —a story to help me demonstrate that I was one of them.

Leading from the Lunch Line

The next morning, I had to cross another Rubicon: the first day of work and my public introduction to Mattel employees. At that meeting, I had to accomplish several things. I had to reassure people that better days were in store, lay out a new vision and mission for the company, and build momentum for the changes ahead.

I needed an icebreaker—a simple yet symbolic story that would help me demonstrate that I was one of them. The story presented itself in the form of my company badge, which was made just before the general meeting. Like every new employee, I'd been marched unceremoniously to the security office, where I had to sit on a stool in my suit and tie for a DMV-style photo. As with all such bureaucratic experiences, this one was vaguely undignified—especially since everyone in the room knew who I was, though I had yet to be introduced. The badge, it seemed to me, provided an opportunity to use another tool: the appeal to common experience.

Coincidentally, the meeting was held in the employee cafeteria. As Alan led me in, I saw 700 or so people sitting in chairs arranged theatre-style and video-conference cameras trained on the podium to transmit my remarks live to similar rooms in Mattel's offices around the world. The moment I was introduced, I took the cordless mike, walked off the platform, and waded out into the audience, where I launched into the story of getting my badge. For five minutes, I poked fun at the entire process: the stool, the camera, saying "cheese," the photo, the plastic badge, and my new friend Alan, that king of all the bureaucratic processes in the company. Though I didn't fully realize it at the time, the badge story offered an ideal symbol for the change that my arrival represented. Besides showing employees that I'd been humbled by a banal process, it also made the badge a focus of my newfound identity—my first step from "food" guy to "toy" guy.

Following the badge story, I set about articulating management's plan to refocus the company by building brands, cutting costs, and developing people. Of course, this last item interested employees most, and as I went on to explain my ideas for an employee-development program, their eyes widened. I didn't know that this was the first time in many years that the CEO had talked about the importance of helping people build careers and rewarding them for a job well done. Having described these plans in some detail, I opened the floor to questions. To my surprise, nearly all of them focused on my personal life—my wife and children's names, the kids' ages, how our move from Chicago was going, where we planned to live, and so on. It was apparent from the nature of the questions and the gracious atmosphere that these employees were hungry for a leader who was down-to-earth. I knew right away that these were my kind of folks.

It was during that first employee meeting that I decided to eat lunch in the cafeteria at every opportunity. For me, the cafeteria is an excellent place to repeat that tried-and-true practice of Management 101: Management by Walking Around. MBWA sends positive messages to employees by revealing your interest in them and their work. At Mattel, where employees had long felt out of touch with management, MBWA has made a difference. I still make an effort to stand in the lunch line instead of having lunch sent up to my office. At first, employees seemed puzzled to see me in the cafeteria, but eventually they became accustomed to my presence. Today employees make appointments to meet me there for lunch; at other times, I arrange group lunches with various departments or teams to talk about what's on people's minds. And

The cafeteria is the ideal place to wield all my favorite management tools.

whenever I find myself without a lunch partner, employees approach me just to say hello. Sometimes they ignore me—and that's good, because it means they really do see me as a coworker.

I have witnessed several positive effects of eating in the cafeteria. First, it has broken down the barriers between managers and their subordinates; some other managers and executives from the upper floors of the building now eat in the cafeteria, too. Second, it's a great place to test new ideas. I've tossed around what I've thought were great ideas only to have them reshaped and improved by my colleagues. Third, it's where I can assess the general mood. I am convinced that I end up learning more from people's questions than they do from my answers. And although I can't eat lunch every day in every Mattel cafeteria around the globe, I communicate regularly with all employees through an e-mail titled "What's on My Mind," in which I share things I've been thinking about and invite employees to respond. I read every one of their messages.

Finally, the cafeteria has proven to be the ideal place to wield all of my favorite management tools at once. The casual feel of the place seems to encourage the frankness, humanity, and honesty I'm attempting to foster. Standing in the lunch line, I can defer to others by asking for their thoughts, observations, and opinions, thus allowing them to teach me. And the cafeteria is one of the few sites in the company where I have an opportunity to share a common, quotidian experience with every other Mattel employee: the noontime meal.

Table Manners

For a new CEO, these metaphorical and actual meals teach important lessons about how to fit into the strange, new world of another company. These lessons hit home early on, when I twice confronted my own false assumptions about Mattel's culture and once confronted an assumption about myself.

My first lesson occurred during my first month on the job, at an off-site meeting with senior management. Before we began the two-day meeting, I wanted to clear the air and answer any questions they still had, so I explained that I would leave the room while questions were gathered, which could then be asked anonymously. When I returned, I said, I would answer every question. I thought we would be finished in half an hour. Several hours later, I was still answering such pointed questions as, "I've heard you are an in-the-trenches manager who listens to the lower levels. Does that mean you'll go around us and make decisions without involving us?" To my chagrin, I discovered that I had completely underestimated not only their wariness but also their ability to read between the lines. I also realized that they had done as much homework on me as I had done on Mattel, which told me I was walking into a sharp team of managers.

Another lesson occurred six months into my tenure, when I was hoping to fill some open positions with talented people I'd worked with over the years. I was absolutely certain that these people could do the job, but whether they would fit into Mattel's culture was another question and not my area of expertise. Enter Alan, who spoke with each candidate. Alan agreed with me about two of my choices, but he explained that the third person was not a good match. I was surprised and disagreed with him, but I deferred to his judgment. Today I realize that Alan was right: My candidate didn't demonstrate a "Mattel first" set of priorities. Moreover, I came to understand that despite my confidence at the time, six months at Mattel wasn't long enough to understand the culture fully.

A third lesson occurred when I realized that even the most important management principles must occasionally bend for the greater good. One of my first tasks at Mattel was to review the annual incentive plan. Though employees expected and deserved an annual bonus, the sales targets had been set so high that there was no way the company could meet them. Given these targets, it was obvious that we would be unable to pay out any bonuses.

This put me in a tough position. On the one hand, it's been my philosophy never to change financial targets once they are set. But on the other hand, I knew that employees needed a bonus—it had been more than two years since they'd hit the targets for one, and if they failed again, they'd feel as if they were being punished for problems that they didn't create. I spent a sleepless night struggling to make a decision. Should I stick to a principle I'd followed strictly throughout my career, or should I make a one-time exception and lower the sales targets, thereby accommodating the small bonus employees needed? If I chose the latter, I ran the risk of appearing to be fiscally undisciplined, which I was not. But if I chose the former, I'd risk losing the faith of the people on whom Mattel's success—and mine—most depended. In the end, I opted to lower the sales goals—and for the first time in two years, employees received bonus checks. In retrospect, this turned out to be the right decision. The employees realized I was on their side, and they redoubled their commitment to our turnaround.

All of these lessons taught me that regardless of whatever talent or management experience I might have developed over the years, the most important thing I could bring to Mattel was a sense of humility and obligation to others. I am certainly obliged to our customers and shareholders, but I am especially obliged to our people.

IN THE EARLY DAYS, of course, there were critical business issues to deal with—not the least of which included selling the Learning Company, tightening capital spending, slashing the dividend, and convincing the financial communities that Mattel was getting back on track. Looking back, I realize how important the people issues were, too. I know now how essential it was for everyone at Mattel to feel, hear, and reach out to me in a human way. Today whenever I mingle with employees— in the elevators, in the hallways, on the grounds of our offices across the country, and in our manufacturing facilities around the world—I rely on my "utensils" of honesty, deference, and recognition of common experience. And I call on all these tools at mealtimes, whether at team-building dinners with senior vice presidents or over sandwiches with employees in the cafeteria. I'm convinced that Mattel's success in pulling out of the dark days has been due to employees' renewed commitment to the company.

This conviction became clear—again—not long ago, when a board member came to Mattel for a visit. As our morning meeting came to an end, he asked me, "Where shall we go for lunch?" When I replied, "Let's go to the cafeteria," he raised an eyebrow. Nevertheless, he followed me downstairs. As we stood in the sandwich line, he had time to take in not just the good food but also the friendly atmosphere. "Great cafeteria you have here, Bob," he said. I smiled at him and thought to myself, "You have no idea."

Jumping Industries: Ten Tips

WHAT DO YOU DO WHEN you are considering a
move from an industry you know well to one you don't
know at all? Here are Bob Eckert's recommendations:

1 **Call on customers**
Without being overly direct, you can learn how the
industry is viewed.

2 **Watch consumers**
For consumer goods manufacturers or retailers, time
spent in the store pays huge dividends.

3 **Find retirees**
Alumni know more about the industry and the company's
culture than anyone else.

4 **Read everything**
The Internet makes it easy to find obscure books and
articles.

5 **Talk to a mentor**
Even though he or she may not know the prospective
industry well, your mentor does have an objective opin-
ion of your abilities and capacity to adapt.

6 **Phone a friend**
I had better results than most of the "Who Wants to Be a
Millionaire" callers.

7 **Keep notes from every conversation**
When you have time to reflect, these notes can help you
put together the puzzle pieces of the new job or industry.

8 **Before taking the job, write down your goals for the
first 100 days**
What do you plan to bring to the new company? What
knowledge can you transfer from the former industry?
What do you need to learn quickly? How will you do it?

9 **Follow your heart**
You can painstakingly write down the pros and cons of the new position, but let your gut feeling be your final guide.

10 **Commit fully**
Once you decide to make the move, always look forward instead of being distracted by the "could haves, would haves, and should haves" of the old job.

Originally published in November 2001
Reprint R0110B

About the Contributors

DR. STEVEN BERGLAS is a management consultant and executive coach who spent twenty-five years on the faculty of Harvard Medical School's Department of Psychiatry and is currently a Visiting Professor at the Marshall School of Business, Lloyd Greif Center for Entrepreneurial Studies, at the University of Southern California. Dr. Berglas specializes in consulting to businesses on the factors that maximize the quality of executives' decision-making, preventing career burnout, and coaching executives who have engaged in self-defeating behavior.

At the time this article was originally published, ROBERT A. ECKERT was the chairman and CEO of Mattel, which is headquartered in El Segundo, California.

At the time this article was originally published, JOSEPH FULLER was the CEO of Monitor Group, a global professional services firm headquartered in Cambridge, Massachusetts.

RAKESH KHURANA is assistant professor of organizational behavior at the Harvard Business School. His book on the CEO labor market, *Searching for a Corporate Savior: The Irrational Quest for Charismatic CEOs* (Princeton University Press, 2002) was described by *Fortune* magazine as "the most important—and timely—management book of 2002."

MICHAEL MACCOBY is an anthropologist and a psycho-analyst. He is also the Founder and President of the Maccoby Group, a management consultancy in Washington, DC. The former director of the Program on Technology, Public Policy, and Human Development at Harvard University's Kennedy School of Government in Cambridge, Massachusetts, Maccoby is the author of *The Leader: A New Face for American Management, The Gamesman: The New Corporate Leaders,* and *Why Work? Motivating the New Workforce.*

LEONARD D. SCHAEFFER is the Chairman and CEO of WellPoint Health Networks in Thousand Oaks, California, one of the nation's largest publicly traded health care companies, with annual revenues exceeding $18 billion. Schaeffer led the recapitalization of WellPoint in 1996, resulting in the creation of America's sixth-largest philanthropy, with a current endowment of more than $4 billion. Previously, Schaeffer served under President Carter as the administrator of the Health Care Financing Administration (HCFA) in the U.S. Department of Health Education and Welfare (now known as the Department of Health and Human Services).

RICHARD S. TEDLOW, Class of 1949 Professor of Business Administration at Harvard Business School in Boston, is the author of *Giants of Enterprise: Seven Business Innovators and the Empires They Built* (HarperBusiness, November 2001). *Giants of Enterprise* was selected by *BusinessWeek* as one of the top 10 books of 2001.

DR. MARGARETHE F. WIERSEMA is a Professor of Strategic Management at the Graduate School of Management at the University of California at Irvine. Professor Wiersema is internationally recognized for her expertise on issues relating to CEOs, executive succession, corporate governance, and corporate strategy and has published extensively on these topics in the premier academic and practitioner journals including the *Harvard Business Review, Strategic Management Journal, Administrative Science Quarterly,* and the *Academy of Management Journal.* In addition, she has presented numerous talks on the topics of executive succession, corporate governance, and corporate strategy. Professor Wiersema received an M.B.A. and Ph.D. in Strategic Management from the Michigan Business School at the University of Michigan.

Index

others, obligation to, 145
outside forces, reliance on,
42–45. *See also* executive
coaching, dangers of;
executive search firms
outsiders, as CEOs. *See also*
leadership transition process
CEO firings and, 23, 29
challenges for, 135–136
charismatic leadership and,
11–14
tips for, 146–147

participative leadership style,
106–110
Patterson, John, 129–130
Paul, the apostle, 3
performance expectations, and
CEO dismissals, 30–31,
33–35
Perot, Ross, 83
Peters, Tom, 96
populist capitalism, 4–5
power, and executive coaches,
65–69
Procter & Gamble, 21
productive narcissists, 76–77
psychological problems, and
executive coaching, 55,
58–59, 69–70
psychotherapy
limits of, 58–59
narcissitic leaders and, 74,
92–93
value of, 69–70

Qwest, 29, 94–95

Raytheon, 37
RBOCs. *See* regional Bell operating companies (RBOCs)
Reagan, Ronald, 7, 17
reformer leadership styles,
111–113
regional Bell operating companies (RBOCs), 81, 94
Reichardt, Carl, 35
Renault, 78
Revlon, 115, 131
Revson, Charles, 115, 118, 120,
126
"robber barons," 127
Rochester Savings Bank, 131
Rockefeller, John D., 76, 127
Roosevelt, Franklin Delano, 75
Rubinstein, Helena, 126

SAS, 96–97
scapegoating
charismatic leaders and, 8
company performance and,
21
Scott, Tom, 127
Seidman, Robert, 111–112
selection process for CEOs
charismatic leaders and,
10–14
factors in, 29–30, 32–33
self-confidence, 131
senior executive team, 48–51
"setting the table," 134, 136
Shapiro, Robert B., 82

160   *Index*